Using
PowerPoint 2019

Kevin Wilson

Elluminet Press

www.elluminetpress.com

Using PowerPoint 2019

Publisher: Elluminet Press
Director: Kevin Wilson
Lead Editor: Steven Ashmore
Technical Reviewer: Mike Taylor, Robert Ashcroft
Copy Editors: Joanne Taylor, James Marsh
Proof Reader: Mike Taylor
Indexer: James Marsh
Cover Designer: Kevin Wilson

eBook versions and licenses are also available for most titles. Any source code or other supplementary materials referenced by the author in this text is available to readers at

www.elluminetpress.com/resources

For detailed information about how to locate your book's resources, go to

www.elluminetpress.com/resources

Table of Contents

About the Author

With over 15 years' experience in the computer industry, Kevin Wilson has made a career out of technology and showing others how to use it. After earning a master's degree in computer science, software engineering, and multimedia systems, Kevin has held various positions in the IT industry including graphic & web design, building & managing corporate networks, training, and IT support.

He currently serves as Elluminet Press Ltd's senior writer and director, he periodically teaches computer science at college in South Africa and serves as an IT trainer in England. His books have become a valuable resource among the students in England, South Africa and our partners in the United States.

Kevin's motto is clear: "If you can't explain something simply, then you haven't understood it well enough." To that end, he has created a series of textbooks, in which he breaks down complex technological subjects into smaller, easy-to-follow steps that students and ordinary computer users can put into practice.

Microsoft PowerPoint

Microsoft PowerPoint allows you to create multimedia presentations that include animation, narration, images, and videos all from a library of pre designed templates or from a blank canvas.

PowerPoint can be used to create presentations for your up coming sales pitch, perhaps you are giving a lecture on a specific subject, teaching, or feeding back information in a meeting. All these can be enhanced using PowerPoint presentations as a visual aid.

To get your message across, you break it down into slides. Think of each slide as a canvas for the pictures, words, and shapes that will help you build your presentation.

You can create slideshows of family photos and holidays/vacations and send to friends.

You can also print out your presentation slides to give to your audience.

PowerPoint offers various features and tools to create, edit and deliver presentations. These tools are all grouped into tabs in a menu system along the top of the screen called a ribbon. You can create presentations made up of slides, containing text, images, audio and videos.

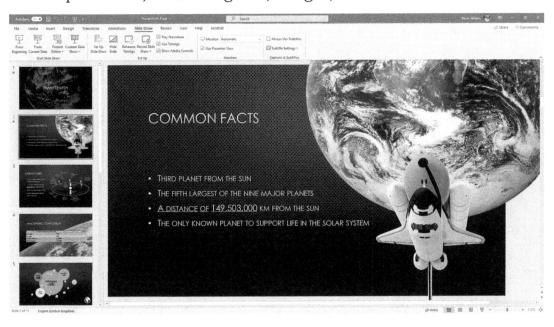

You can link your laptop or tablet to a digital projector or large TV.

Getting Started with PowerPoint

In this section, we'll take a look at starting PowerPoint and have a look at the different parts of the screen.

Getting Started

You can start PowerPoint by searching for it using Cortana's search field on your task bar. Type in 'powerpoint'. Then click 'PowerPoint ' desktop app as highlighted below.

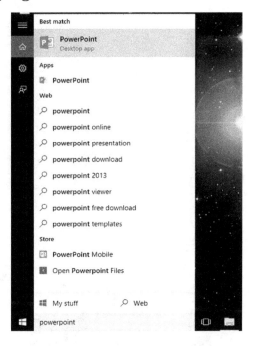

Create a Shortcut

To make things easier, you can pin the PowerPoint icon to your task bar. I find this feature useful. To do this, right click on the PowerPoint icon on your taskbar and click 'pin to taskbar'.

This way, PowerPoint is always on the taskbar whenever you need it.

Chapter 2: Getting Started with PowerPoint

Once PowerPoint has started, you'll land on the home screen. On the home screen, you'll see recently used templates along the top, and your most recently saved presentations listed underneath.

To begin, click 'new' to start. Here you'll find templates and pre-designed themes to help you create your presentation.

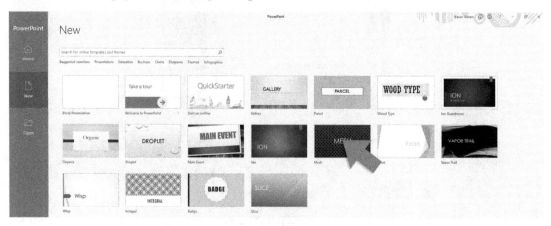

On some templates, you can choose colour schemes and styles for fonts and text. The mesh template has 4 different colour schemes which affect the colour of the text. Click on one and click create.

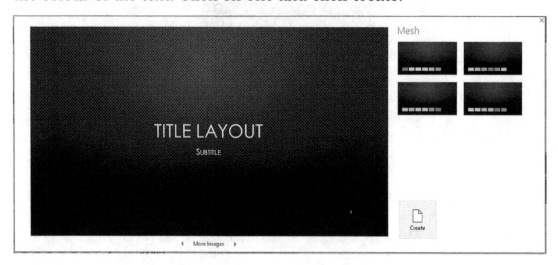

Lets take a look at PowerPoint's main screen. Along the top are your ribbon menu. This is where you'll find all your tools for creating your slides.

Down the left hand side, you'll see a thumbnail list of all your slides in the presentation, in the centre of the screen you'll see the currently selected slide you're working on.

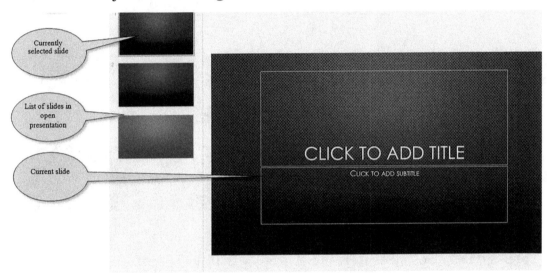

Along the bottom right you'll see icons to add presenter notes and comments. Adjust the view - ie how PowerPoint displays your slides on your screen. You can have normal view, slide sorter view and reading view. The next icon along runs your presentation - use this when presenting to your audience.

You can also adjust the zoom. This zooms in and out of the current slide. The last icon auto fits the current slide to the same size as the screen.

Speaker notes. These aren't visible to your audience, but will show up on the presenter view while you give your presentation.

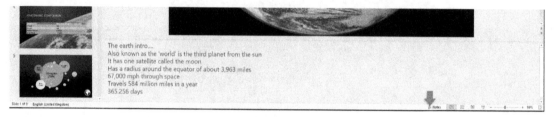

Slide sorter view. Click and drag slides to reorder.

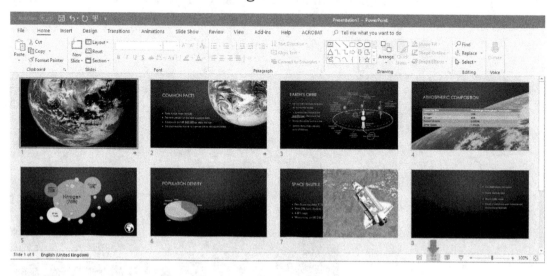

Normal view. Best view for designing your PowerPoint presentations.

The Ribbon

All tools in PowerPoint are organised into a ribbon which is divided into ribbon tabs, each containing a specific set of tools.

The Home Ribbon

All tools to do with text formatting, for example, making text bold, changing fonts, and the most common tools for text alignment, and formatting.

You'll also find your cut, copy & paste functions, as well as shortcuts for adding shapes, and inserting new slides.

The Insert Ribbon

All tools to do with inserting photos, graphics, 3D models, tables, charts, sounds, or movies. You can also insert equations, word art and smart art using this ribbon.

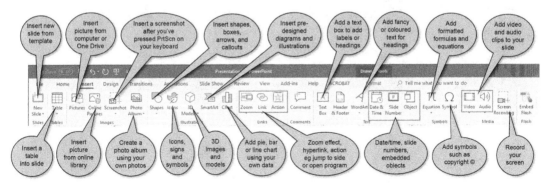

You can create zoom effects to help emphasise an illustration on your slide, as well as screen recordings, and on click actions.

The Design Ribbon

All tools to do with the look of your slide, eg, the slide background.

The Transitions Ribbon

All tools to add effects to show as slides change from one to the next.

The Animations Ribbon

All tools to add slide transitions and adding effects to text boxes, images and headings.

The Slide Show Ribbon

All tools to do with setting up your slide show and running your presentation.

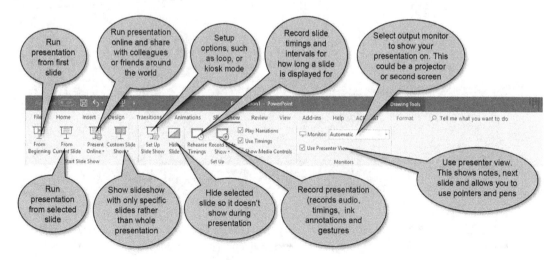

File Backstage

If you click 'File' on the top left of your screen, this will open up what Microsoft call the backstage.

Backstage is where you open or save presentations, print, export or share presentations, as well as options, Microsoft account and preference settings.

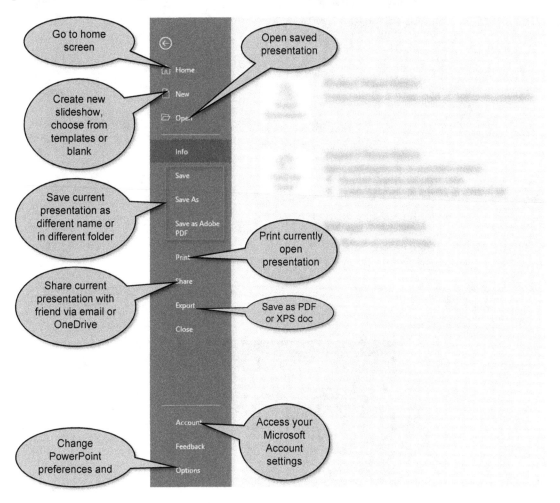

You can also change your Microsoft Account settings, log in and activate your Microsoft Office, change PowerPoint's preferences and so on.

Normal View

Normal view is the default view and the best way to design and develop your presentation. It lists all your slides down the left hand side, with the selected slide displayed in the centre of the screen for you to work on.

Outline View

The outline view, shows you a list of your slide's text, rather than a thumbnail view of the slide. You wont see any images or graphics inserted into any of your slides on the left hand side.

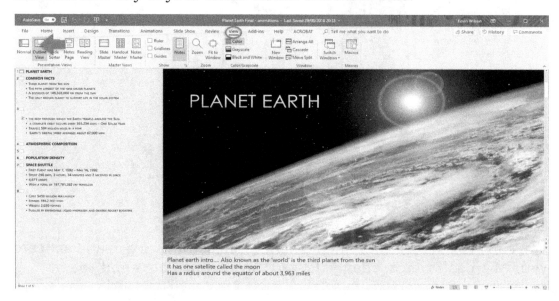

Slide Sorter View

The slide sorter view shows you a thumbnail list of all your slides in the presentation.

As the name suggests, it allows you to easily see all your slides and makes it easier for you to put them into the correct order.

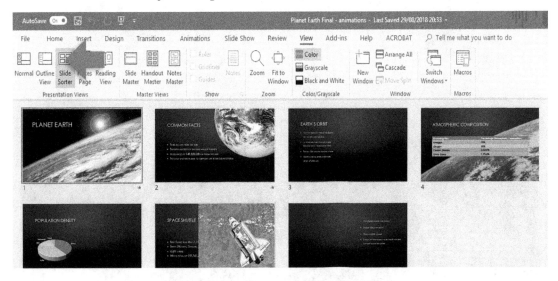

As well as hide certain slides you may not need in a particular session when presenting. To do this, right click the slide, then from the popup menu select 'hide slide'.

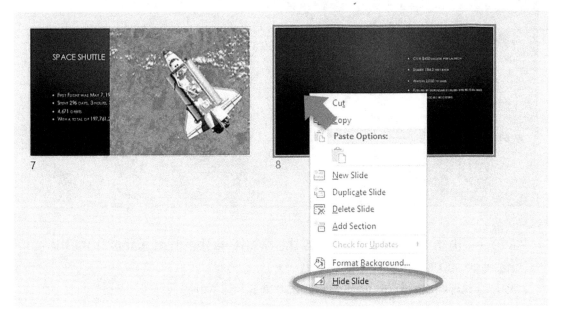

Hidden slides are greyed out with the slide number crossed out. To un-hide the slide, right click on the slide, and click 'hide slide' again.

Note Page View

Note page view, allows you to see the slide with the notes associated with that slide.

Select the view ribbon and click 'notes page'.

The notes view makes it easier to add notes to each slide, or to review notes already added.

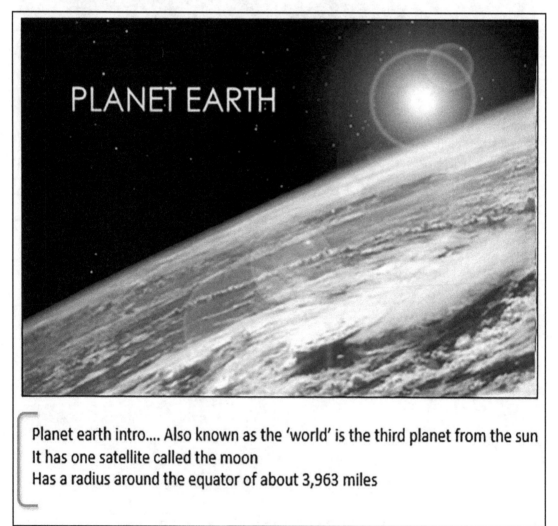

Planet earth intro.... Also known as the 'world' is the third planet from the sun
It has one satellite called the moon
Has a radius around the equator of about 3,963 miles

Reading View

To switch to reading view, select the view ribbon and click 'reading view'.

This view allows you to play your PowerPoint presentation slideshow within the PowerPoint window.

Building Presentations

In this section, we'll take a look at building a simple presentation.

Before we begin, throughout this section, we will be using the resource files.

You can download these files from

`www.elluminetpress.com/ms-ppt`

Go down to the files section and click the icons to download the documents to the documents folder on your PC.

Creating a New Presentation

When you start PowerPoint you'll see the home screen. Here you'll see your most used PowerPoint templates across the top of the screen, underneath that, you'll see a list of your most recently opened presentations.

PowerPoint has a wealth of templates and themes for all sorts of different types of presentations. To use the templates, select 'new' from the orange strip along the left hand side of the screen.

To begin creating our presentation, for this example double click on the 'mesh' template.

Chapter 3: Building Presentations

This will open up a blank presentation with this template for you to add your content.

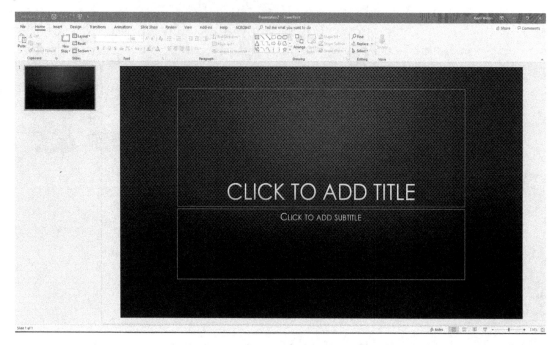

You can search for templates for the presentation you are creating. To do this, use the search field at the top of the screen.

Type in what you're looking for and hit enter.

Select a template from the search results.

Designing a Slide

Lets begin by adding the title to our first slide

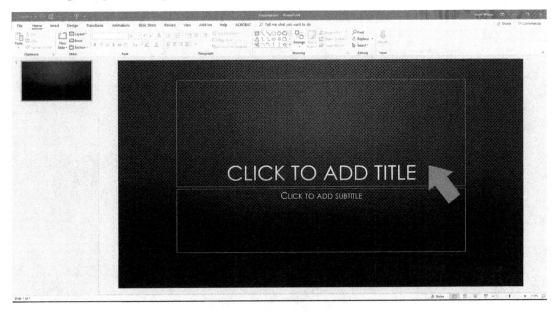

On your slide, click where it says 'click to add title'. This is a place holder for you to enter a title.

Enter the title 'Planet Earth'.

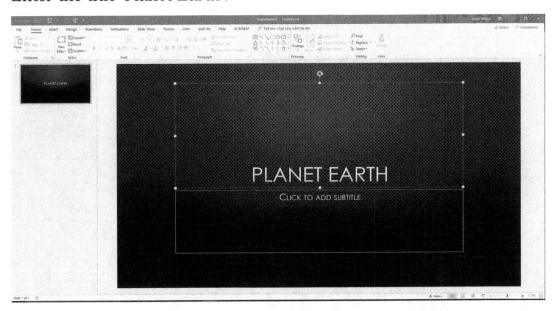

In this example, we won't be adding a subtitle, but you can add one if you want to.

Lets add some images to spice our title slide up a bit.

Adding a New Slide

To continue building our presentation we need additional slides to show our information.

To add a new slide, go to your home ribbon and click on icon 'New Slide'. Make sure you click on the text to reveal the drop down menu.

From the drop down menu, select 'title and content' because we want a title on the slide but also we want to add some information in bullet points.

To add your text and titles, just click in the text boxes and start typing your information as shown below.

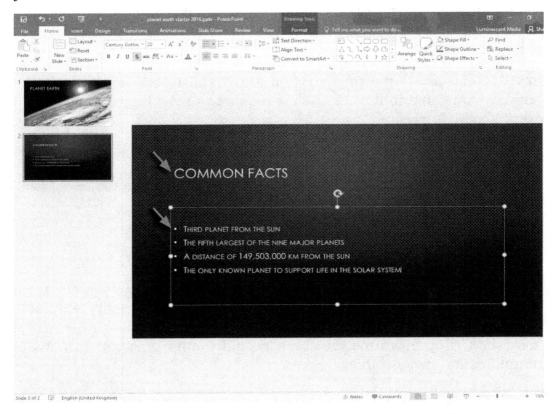

You can make text bigger by selecting it. Drag and highlight the text. From your home ribbon select the increase font size icon.

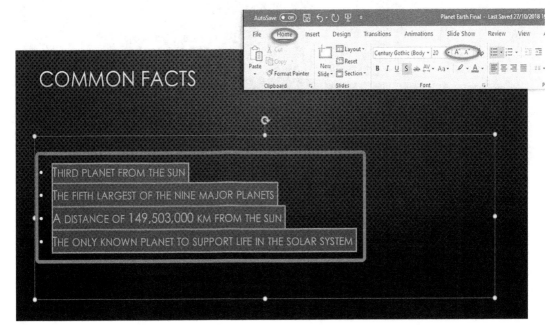

Slide Masters

Slide masters allow you to create layouts and templates that are common to all your slides, so you don't have to make those changes to each slide.

Say you are creating a presentation and want a company logo on the bottom, you can add it to your slide master and the logo will appear on every slide you create.

To edit your slide masters, go to your view ribbon and click 'slide master'.

The larger slide listed down the left hand side is your master for all slides. The smaller ones are masters for individual slide templates such as 'title slides' or 'title and content' slides. These appear in the 'new slide' drop down menu. You can split them up so you can create templates for specific slides.

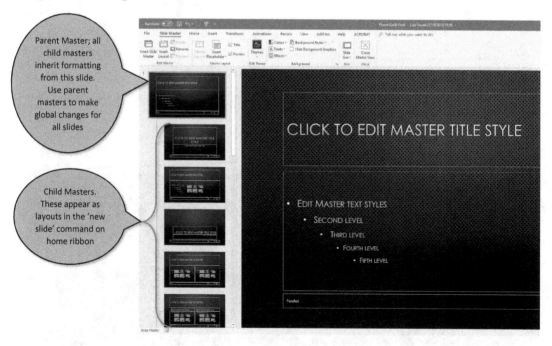

This way, you can have consistent layouts for all your title slides and all your content slides, without having to change the size of the title or position of text or the font every time you insert a new slide.

In this simple example, I am going to add the company logo to the bottom right of every slide. To do this, click on the larger master slide in the list on the left hand side.

Open your file explorer and navigate to your pictures folder, or the folder where the picture you want is saved. Click and drag your image onto the master slide.

You may need to resize your picture and position it in the correct place.

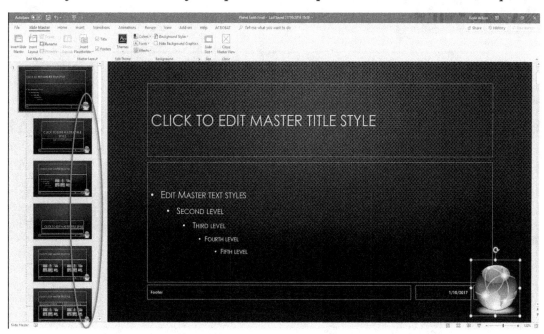

Notice, when you add the logo to the larger slide, it appears on the smaller slides too. This is because the smaller slides inherit their formatting from the larger slide (the larger slide being the parent master slide).

When you're finished click 'close master view'.

Adding Notes

You can add speakers notes to your slides. These notes appear on the presenter view when running your presentation. They can also appear on printed handouts.

First reveal the notes pane. The notes pane is located at the bottom of your screen, but is usually hidden by default. To reveal the pane, click on the dividing line just above the scroll bar, illustrated below with the red arrow. You'll notice your mouse cursor change to a double headed arrow.

Then drag your mouse upwards to reveal the notes pane. You can add speakers notes, bullet points to help you when you're presenting.

These notes will appear on your presenter view, when you run your presentation.

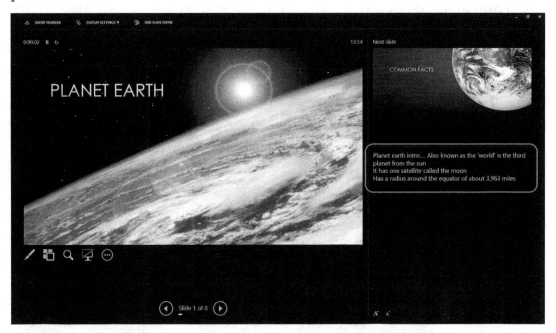

You can also include your notes in printed slide handouts. Go to FILE, then select print. Change the option, circled below, to 'Notes Pages'.

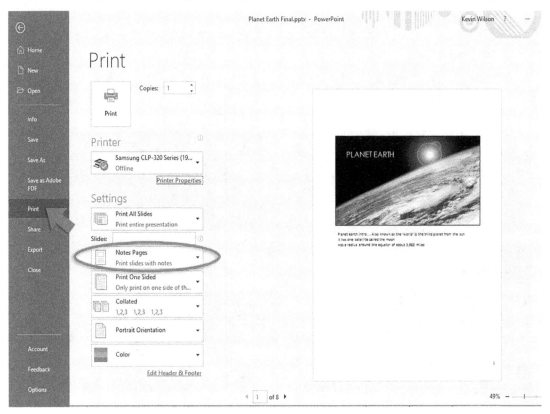

Changing the Slide Order

You can easily change the order or the slides in your presentation. To do this, on the left hand side of your screen, click and drag the slide thumbnails.

You'll see the other slides shift out the way. Drop the slide into the position you want.

Opening a Saved Presentation

If PowerPoint is already open you can open previously saved presentations by clicking the FILE menu on the top left of your screen.

From the orange bar on the left hand side click 'open', then click 'OneDrive - Personal'.

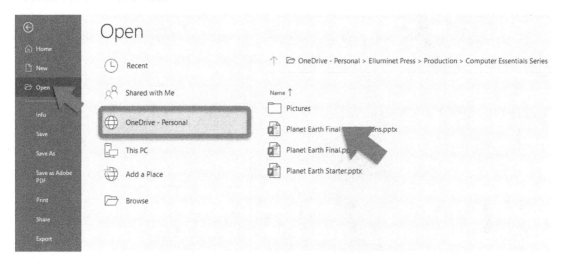

From the list, select the presentation you want to open. The presentation from the previous project was saved as 'planet earth.pptx', so this is the one I am going to open here.

For convenience, instead of searching through your OneDrive, PowerPoint lists all your most recently opened Presentations. You can view these by clicking 'Recent' instead of 'OneDrive - Personal'.

Your latest files will be listed first.

Double click the file name to open it.

Saving your Presentation

Click the small disk icon on the top left of the screen. If this is a new presentation that hasn't been saved before, PowerPoint will ask you where you want to save it. Save all your work onto your OneDrive.

Click OneDrive Personal.

then enter a name for your presentation in the field indicated by the red arrow below.

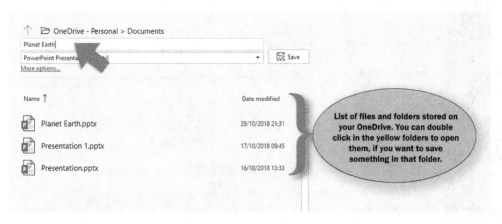

List of files and folders stored on your OneDrive. You can double click in the yellow folders to open them, if you want to save something in that folder.

When you have done that click save.

Save as a Different Format

To save your presentation in a different format, with your presentation open, click FILE.

From the backstage view, click 'Save As'.

Select the folder you want to save your file in, eg, documents folder on your OneDrive.

Give your document a name, then underneath, click the down arrow and select a format. In this example, I am going to save the PowerPoint presentation as a PDF.

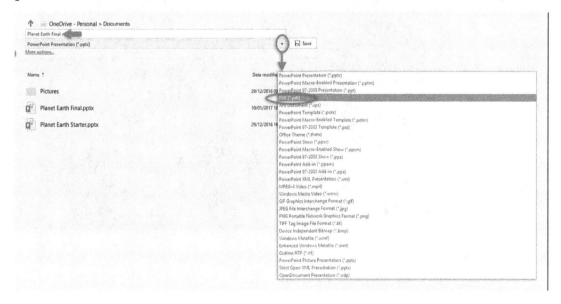

This is useful if you want to send a copy to someone that doesn't use Windows or have PowerPoint installed. Note with a PDF, you won't see all your animations or transitions in the file.

Click 'save' when you're done.

Chapter 3: Building Presentations

When you view the PDF version of your presentation, you'll see all the text and graphics.

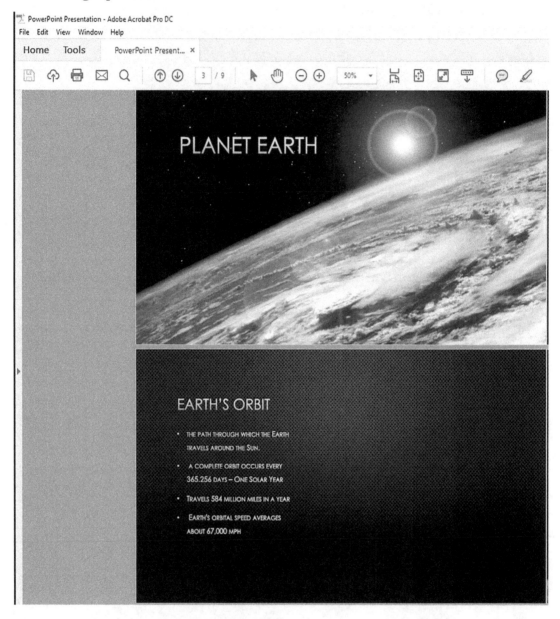

You can also save as a video. Use MPEG-4/MP4 video for Macs, Windows, Tablets, and Phones. Use Windows Media Video (WMV) if you're only using Windows based machines.

If you save your presentation as a video, you'll get all your transitions and animations saved along with any timings and voice recordings you have done. If you haven't, you'll get the default timings for each slide transition and animation. The video presentation will run automatically, you won't be able to click to advance any slides etc.

Print your Slides

To print your slides, click FILE on the top left hand corner of the screen, then select print.

In the screen below select the correct printer and number of copies you want.

Then select how you want the slides to print out. Click where it says 'Full Page Slides'. 'Full Page Slides' prints out one slide per page and can be useful in some situations. If you are printing handouts, it makes sense to print more than one slide per page.

You'll see a pop up menu appear with some layout options for how to print out the slides on the page.

I usually select '3 slides', as it provides space for the audience to take notes on any particular slide.

You can then handout a copy of your slides to your audience so they can follow your presentation as you speak and take notes. I find this the most useful way to print slides.

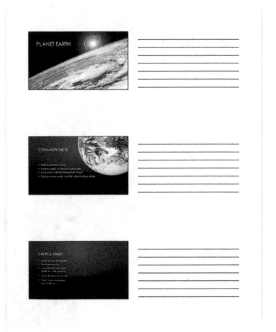

If you just wanted the slides, you could also get six slides on a page. Just choose 'six horizontal slides' instead of '3 slides'.

'Horizontal' means, the slides appear across the page rather than down the page. Notice how the slides are numbered above.

Sometimes it is useful to select 'black and white' or greyscale printing if you do not have a colour printer.

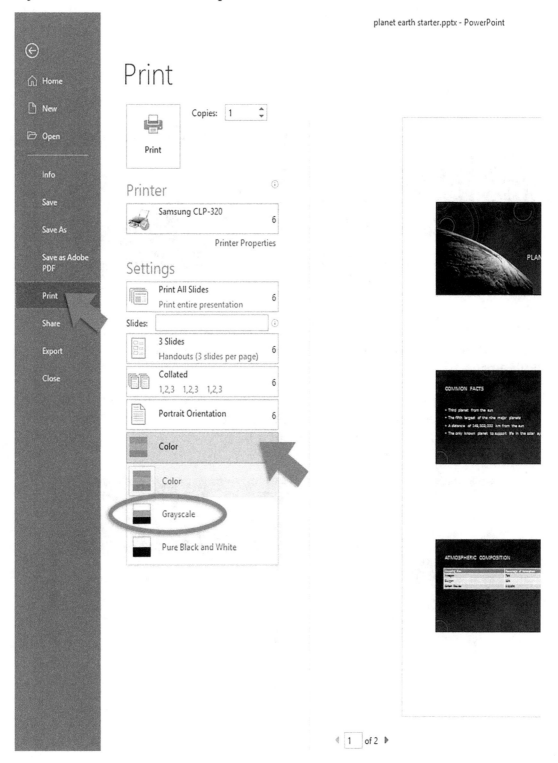

Click the print icon to print your presentation.

Online Collaboration

A new feature that allows users to share their work with others. In the demo below, the user on the laptop has shared the PowerPoint presentation with the user on the tablet.

In the top right of PowerPoint's main screen, there is a share button. You can share any document you are working on with friends and colleagues.

If you want to share the presentation you are working on, click on the share button and enter their email address. Click the contacts icon next to the address field to add names from your contacts. Double click on each name in the address book list to add.

Select 'can edit' to allow people to make changes to your presentation. If you don't want people to make changes, change this option to 'can view'.

When the other person checks their email, on the tablet in this demonstration, they will receive a message inviting them to open the presentation you just shared.

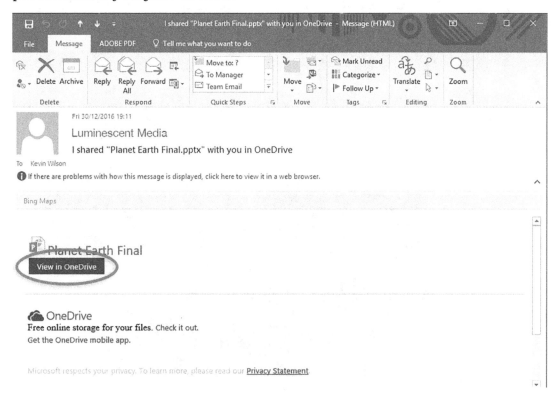

Click 'view in OneDrive', in the email message. The presentation will open in a web browser. Make sure you click 'sign in' on the top right of the screen and enter your Microsoft Account details when prompted.

Once you have signed in, click 'Edit Presentation', then click 'edit in PowerPoint'

Chapter 3: Building Presentations

This will download the document and open it up in PowerPoint installed on your computer (the tablet in this demo).

Here, the user on the tablet can start editing the presentation. As an example, they're going to add a bullet point to the list.

You'll be able to see who is editing what, indicated with a user icon on the top right of the text boxes, circled below.

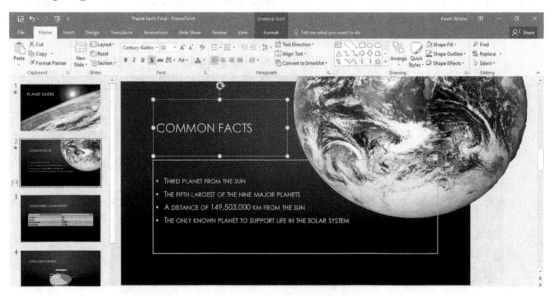

We can see here on the laptop screen, that the user on the tablet is editing the bottom text box.

Slide Themes

You can select from a variety of themes. To do this select the 'design' ribbon. In the middle of the ribbon, you'll see some themes to choose from. Click the small down arrow on the right hand side of the 'themes' section to expand the selection.

Adding Graphics

In this section, we'll take a look at adding images, icons, smartart and shapes

Before we begin, throughout this section, we will be using the resource files.

You can download these files from

www.elluminetpress.com/ms-ppt

Go down to the files section and click the icons to download the documents to the documents folder on your PC.

Adding Images

You can add images or photographs from your computer, for example, photos you have taken. Or you can add images from Office's online library.

From your PC

The easiest way to add an image to your slide, is to first find the image in your pictures library from file explorer. The icon is on your task bar.

Open up your pictures library, then drag and drop the image onto your open slide, as shown below.

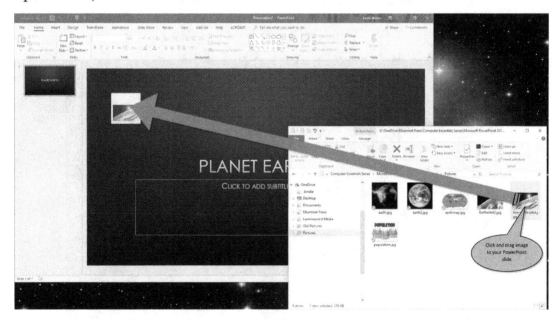

You may need to move your explorer window over to the side if it covers your PowerPoint presentation.

Online Images

You can also add pictures from Office's online library. From your insert ribbon, click 'online pictures'

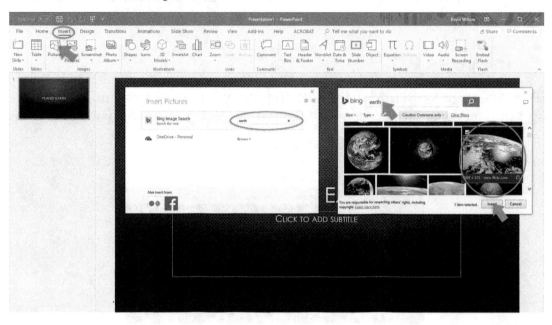

From the dialog box that appears, type your search into the Bing images field and press enter.

From the search results, click the image you want, then click 'insert'.

Now you can place your image and resize it to fit on your slide.

Design Ideas

This is a handy new feature, and appears whenever you insert an image into your slide. PowerPoint will generate some ideas on how to arrange the image you have just inserted into your slide. If you see a design you like, just click on the thumbnail, listed down the right hand side.

This is a quick way to format and arrange images on your slides.

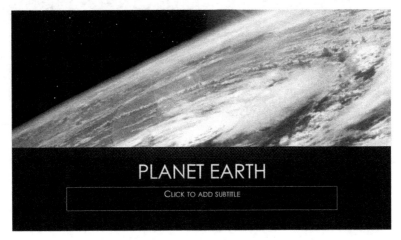

If you don't choose any of the design ideas, you can arrange the image on the slide yourself.

Resizing Images

If you click on your image, you will notice a border surrounding it.

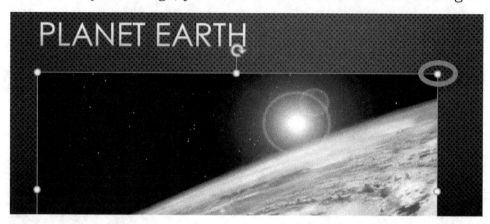

In each corner and along the sides you will notice little white dots.

These are resize handles. You can click and drag these to resize your image.

To resize the image, click and drag the resize handles until the image is the size you want.

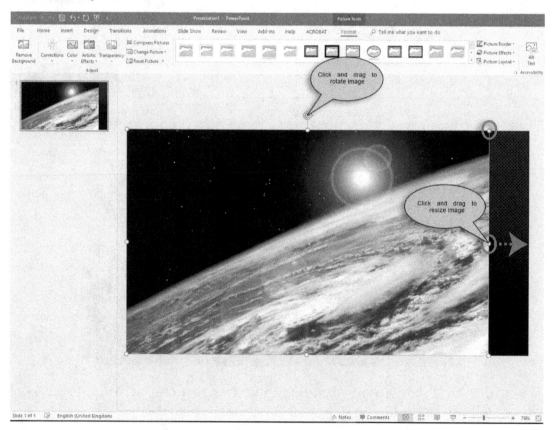

Image Arrangement

You will notice that when you have resized the image, it covers the title. This is because PowerPoint constructs slides using layers. So the title "Planet Earth" will be on one layer, and the image will be on another layer. Now, because the image was inserted after the title, the image layer is on top of the title layer. We want the title layer on top.

We can adjust this by changing the arrangement.

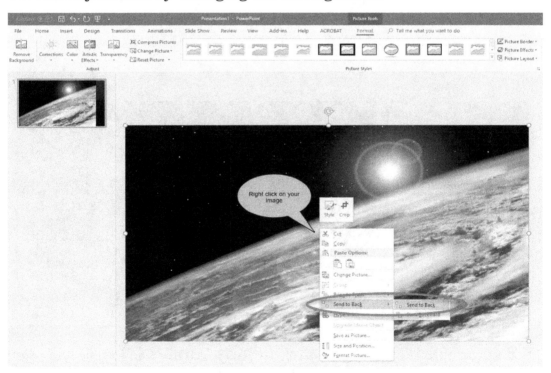

We want to put the image behind the title, so it's in the background on the slide. To do this, right click on your image and from the pop up menu, select 'send to back'.

You will see the image drop behind the text layer.

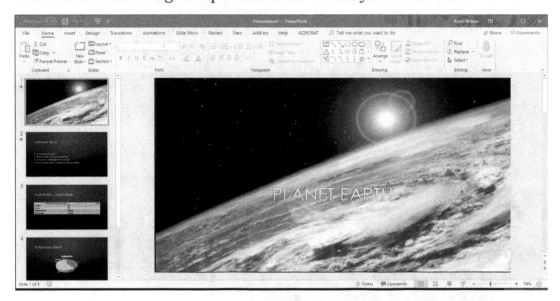

This is useful if you have a lot of images and text that you need to lay out on your slide.

You can now type the title 'Planet Earth' in the text box, and drag it to the desired position on the slide.

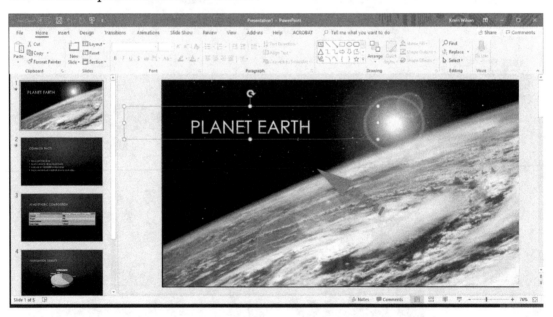

In my example, I'm going to put the title in the top left of the slide against the black. To drag the title text box, when you click on it, you'll see a box appear around the title text box. Click and drag the dotted line surrounding the title, to move your image.

Adding Objects

PowerPoint has a large library of objects you can add to your slides. There are speech bubbles, circles, squares, lines, arrows, stars and a whole lot more to choose from.

Shapes

To insert shapes, go to your insert ribbon and click 'shapes'. From the drop down menu you'll see a whole variety of shapes you can insert.

For this example, I am going to add a cloud shape to the atmosphere slide in my presentation. A cloud could represent the air, as this slide is illustrating. Inside the cloud or the air we could show the different gases.

So use the shapes to compliment and illustrate your slides.

You can change the fill colour of the shape and the outline. To change the fill colour, click on the shape and select your format ribbon. Click 'shape fill' and from the drop down, select a colour.

You can change the border of your shape in a similar fashion. Click your shape and from the format ribbon, select 'shape outline'.

From the drop down, select a colour. Then go further down the menu and select 'weight'. This is the thickness of the border. From the slide out select a border thickness.

Icons

Icons make nice little decorations and illustrations for your slides. You can use them as logos, or to illustrate a point.

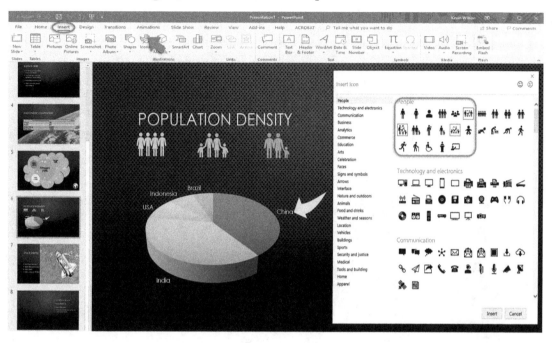

Here I'm using an arrow to point to China for having the largest population, and adding some icons of people to illustrate population.

You can change the colours of your icons. To do this, click on an icon on your slide, then from the format ribbon, select 'graphics fill'.

Select a colour from the drop down menu.

SmartArt

SmartArt allows you to create info graphics, charts and so on. There are a lot of different types of pre-designed templates to choose from.

First, insert a new slide, or select the slide you want the SmartArt to appear. To insert SmartArt, go to your insert ribbon and click 'SmartArt'.

From the dialog box that appears, select a design. In this example, I am trying to illustrate the composition of gasses in the atmosphere, so I'm going to choose the circle design below that looks like gas molecules.

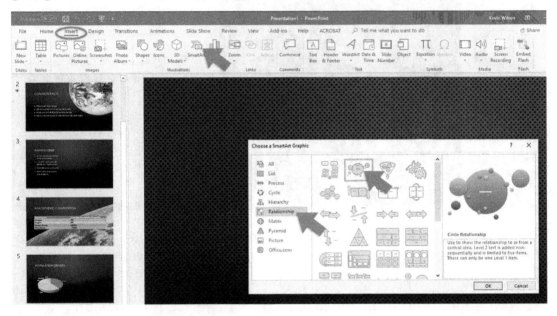

To edit the information, click in the text fields and enter your own data.

You can also change the design of the graphic. For example, change the layout, colour, add some shadows?

Lets change the colour of the 'other gasses' circle. To do this, click on the circle

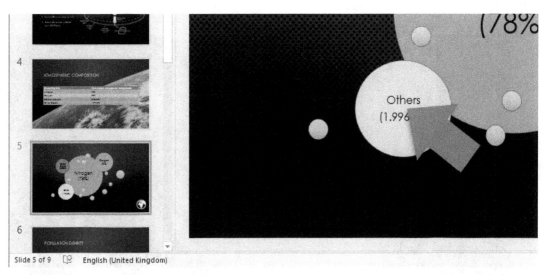

Select the format ribbon under 'smartart tools'.

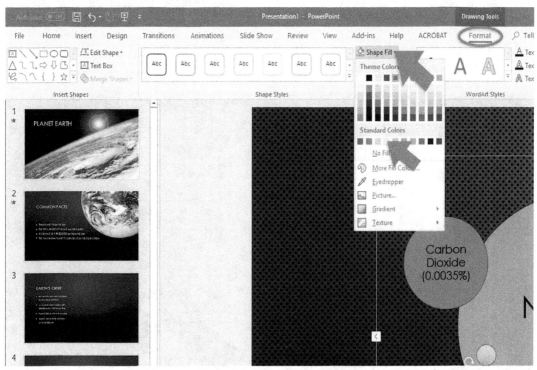

From the format ribbon, click 'shape fill'. Select a colour from the drop down menu. I'm going to colour this one yellow.

Try changing the colours of the other circles.

How about some shadows to separate the circles from each other and add a bit of depth to the graphic.

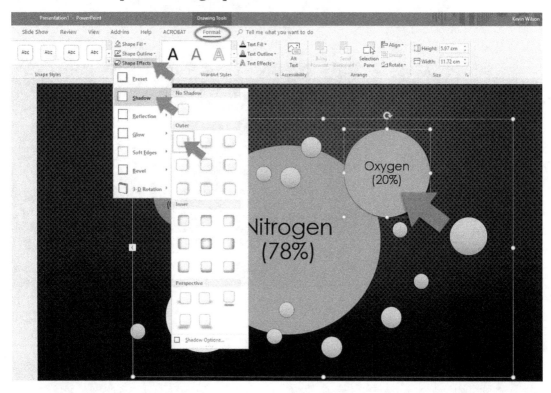

Do the same on some of the other circles. Try some of the other effects too. What about a glow?

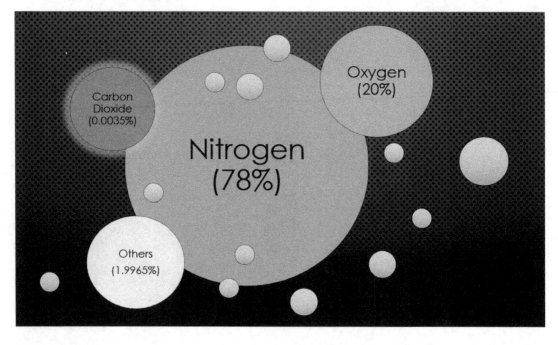

Experiment.

There are also some pre set styles that you can use to format your SmartArt graphic.

To do this, click on your SmartArt graphic on the slide.

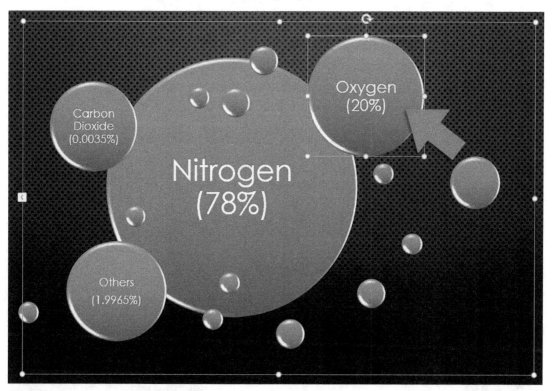

Select the 'design' ribbon under 'SmartArt tools. In the centre of your ribbon, you'll see some styles. Click on one of the icons to select the style.

Try different ones to see what effect they have on the SmartArt graphic on your slide.

Adjusting Images

Sometimes it helps to make some minor adjustments to your photographs or images to make them blend into your slide a little better. You can change the brightness, contrast and colours of the images. You can do all this by experimenting with the adjustments on the format ribbon.

For example. If we add another slide with the photograph of planet earth, the photo has a black background. We can make a few adjustments to this image to make it blend into the slide a little better.

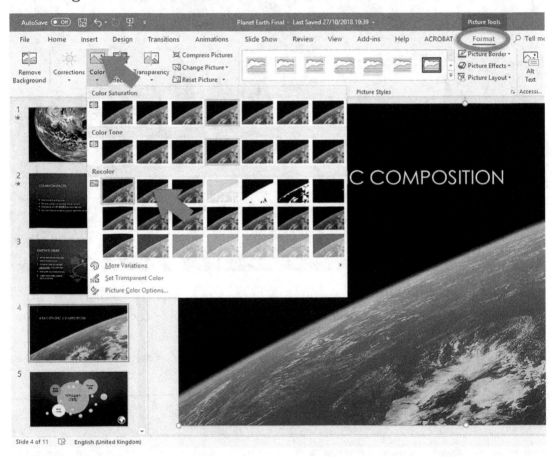

Click on the image on the slide and then click the format ribbon. On the format ribbon go to the adjustment section on the left hand side.

From the drop down menu, you can select 'color' if you want to change the colour blending of the image, eg select a grey tint to match the background theme of the slide.

You can also do the same for other corrections such as brightness and contrast. Do this by selecting 'corrections' from the format ribbon instead of 'color'.

Removing Image Backgrounds

This works best on images that don't have complex or crowded backgrounds.

Instead of seeing the black background from the image, it would be better to use the slide background itself, rather than covering it up.

To remove the background, make sure your image is selected and click 'remove background' from the format ribbon.

This will highlight all the bits PowerPoint is going to remove from the image in dark purple. You will also notice a box surrounding the area.

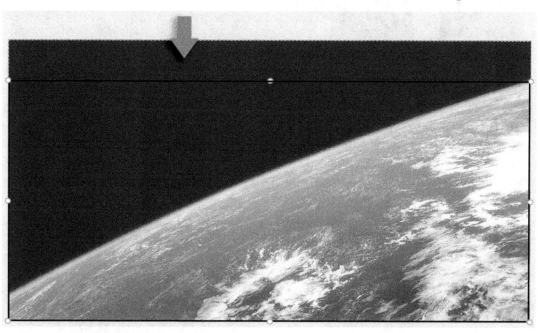

Resize this box by clicking and dragging the resize handles until the box surrounds the area of the image you want to keep as shown above. In this case, around the earth.

Once you have done this click 'keep changes'.

Notice you can now see the slide background instead of the black background on the image.

If your image is a bit more complex and doesn't have a solid background, such as this one of the shuttle, we'll need to tweak the purple mask a bit. After we align the mask box around the shuttle, if you look closely, you'll see that the purple mask has spilled over onto the edges of the wings.

You can mark these areas of the image you don't want PowerPoint to mask out. To do this, click 'mask areas to keep'.

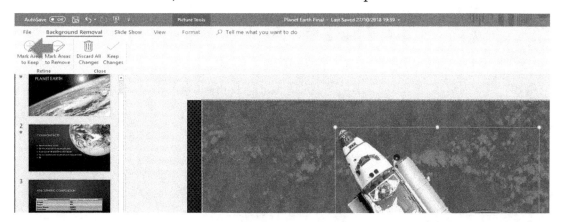

On your image, draw a line across the bit of the image you want to keep. In this case, the edges of the wings. Shown below.

Once you've done that, you'll see the purple mask disappear from the edges of the wings.

Remember, anything highlighted in purple will be removed.

Click 'keep changes', when you're finished.

Charts and Tables

In this section, we'll take a look at creating charts and adding tables to present your data.

Before we begin, throughout this section, we will be using the resource files.

You can download these files from

`www.elluminetpress.com/ms-ppt`

Go down to the files section and click the icons to download the documents to the documents folder on your PC.

Insert a Table

We are going to add a table to a new slide. In this example I have added a new slide with 'title and content'. You can also add a table from the insert ribbon.

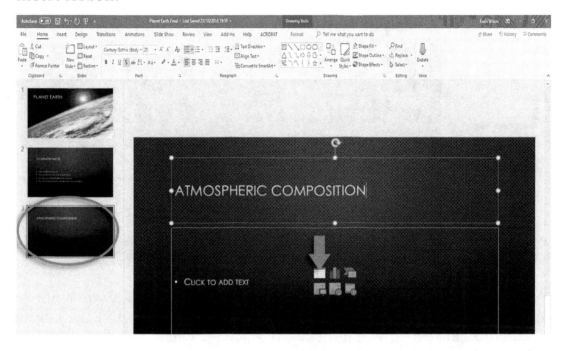

To add a table to this slide, just click the table icon from the template as indicated above. In the dialog box that appears, enter the number of columns and rows. This table is going to have 2 columns.

Once you have done that, enter the data into your table. Press the tab key to move between cells of the table. Don't worry about the number of rows, a new row will be inserted at the end of each row when entering your data - just press tab.

Chapter 5: Charts and Tables

You can also insert a table directly. To do this, go to your insert ribbon and click 'table'.

You can move or resize the table. If you click on the table, you'll notice an outline appear around the table with small dots around the edges. These are called resize handles and you can click and drag them to resize your table.

If you click on the edge line of the table and drag your mouse, you can move your table to the desired position on your slide.

Formatting Tables

To do basic formatting, select the table with your mouse and click your design ribbon.

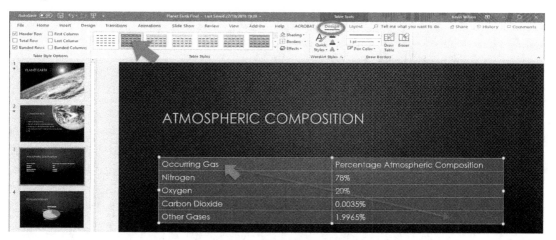

From here you can add some borders, change the shading or add an effect.

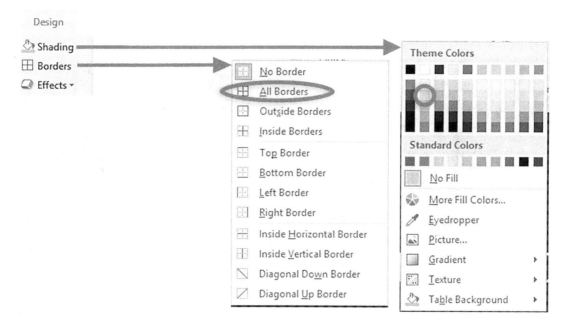

Click 'shading' and add a background colour to the cells. Since the slide is mostly grey, I'm going to choose a lighter grey to compliment the slide colour.

Then click borders, and select 'all borders' to put a border around all cells. You can also select individual cells or groups of cells and add borders to those to emphasise different parts of the table.

Chapter 5: Charts and Tables

You can adjust the border thickness using the 'draw borders' section of the design ribbon. Click the drop down circled below and from the menu, select a thickness.

Finally click 'effects'. Select the type of effect you want (shadow or reflection effects work well). In the example, I am going to add a reflection effect to the table. Go down to 'reflection' and from the slide out, select the type of reflection effect.

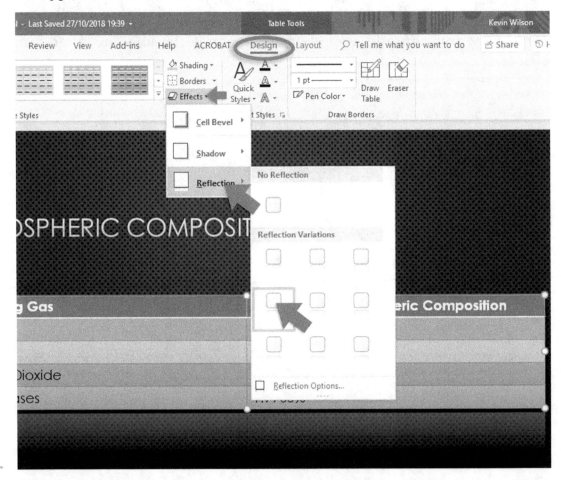

Try experiment with some of the other borders, shadings and effects using these controls.

Table Themes

You can format your table using PowerPoint's pre-designed themes. This makes formatting your table quick and easy.

Click on the table then select the Design ribbon.

Along the centre of the Design ribbon you will see a number of pre sets. Click the small down arrow at the bottom right to expand the selections, circled above.

Click on a design to apply it to the table.

You can experiment with the designs by clicking on these and see how they look.

PowerPoint will automatically format the table using the colours and shadings in the themes.

Add a Chart

We are going to add a chart to a new slide. In this example I have added a new slide with 'title and content'

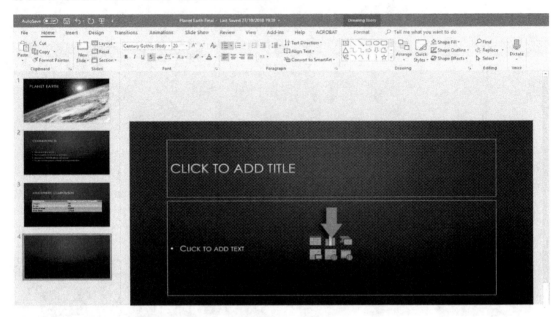

On the slide template, click the chart icon shown above. From the dialog box that appears, select the type of chart you want. In this example, I am going to use a nice 3D pie chart.

Click OK when you are done.

You'll see a spreadsheet like table open up where you can add some data. Enter the data in table shown below.

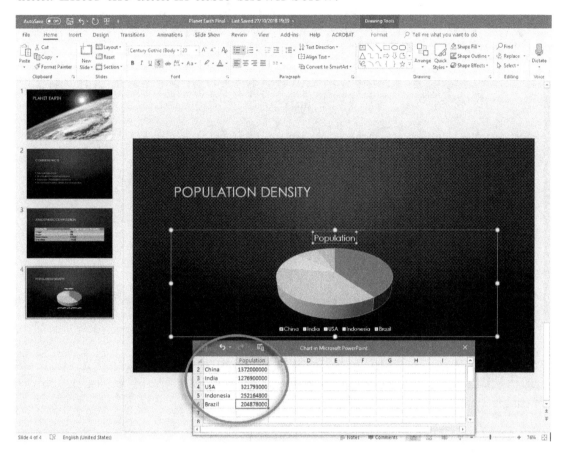

As you enter your data, you'll notice PowerPoint begins to construct your chart.

Remember when constructing your charts, **Column A** is the **X axis** on your chart, **Column B** is the **Y axis**.

Formatting Charts

PowerPoint has a few chart formatting tools to take note of. First click on your chart to select it, you'll notice two new ribbons appear: design and format.

Lets have a look at the design ribbon. Note that there are actually two design ribbons. Make sure you select the ribbon under 'chart tools'.

From here, you can do most of your basic chart formatting such as adding titles, editing your chart data and apply chart styles to make your charts look more visually appealing.

Chart Titles

To a chart title, click on your chart and select the design ribbon. From the design ribbon, click 'add chart element'. Go down to 'chart title' and from the slide out click 'above chart'.

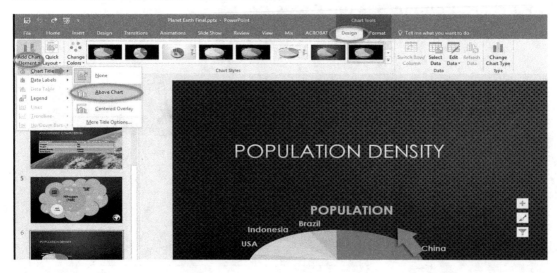

Data Labels

Data labels are the labels that describe what the elements of the chart represent. You can either label each element of the chart or use a chart legend.

Click on your chart.

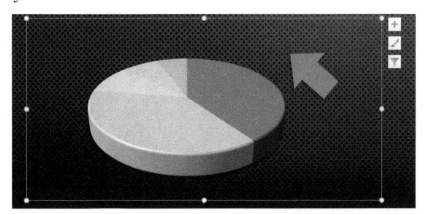

Select 'add chart element' from the design ribbon. From the drop down menu, go down to 'data labels' and from the slide out, click 'data callout' or 'outside end'.

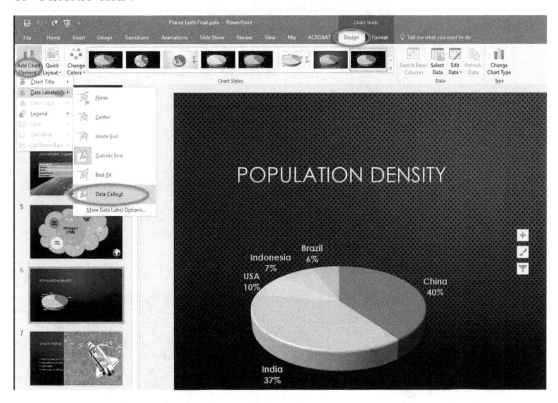

This tells PowerPoint where to position your labels.

Chart Legends

Chart legends are good for explaining what the different parts of your chart represent.

To add a legend to your chart, click on your chart and select your design ribbon, then click 'add chart element'.

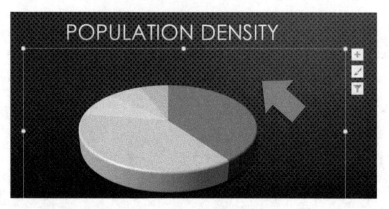

From the drop down menu, go down to 'legend' and from the slide out, click on the position you want the legend.

On the right is usually a good place.

Edit Chart Data

To edit your chart data, click on your chart to select it.

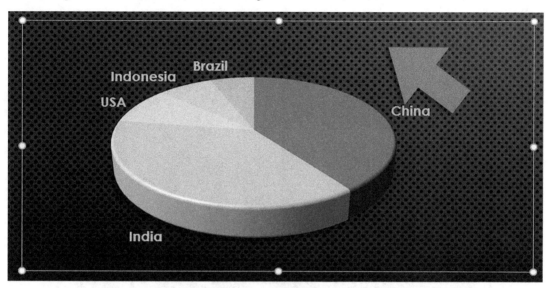

Select your design ribbon under 'chart tools'. Click on 'edit data'. If you get a drop down menu, select 'edit data' again.

You'll see a spreadsheet like window open up with the data used to generate your chart.

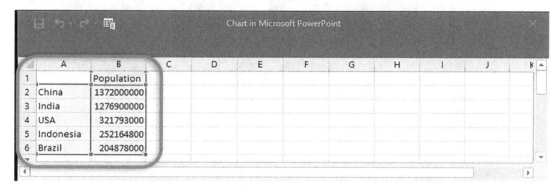

You can edit the data or add to the data from here and PowerPoint will automatically update your chart accordingly.

Chart Styles

You can style your charts pretty quickly using the style options on your design ribbon.

First, click your chart to select it.

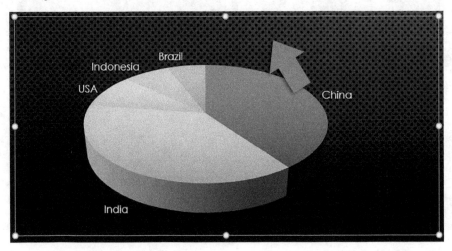

Go to the 'design' ribbon under 'chart tools'. On the centre of your design ribbon, you'll see some chart styles. Click on one of the thumbnail icons to apply a style to your chart.

PowerPoint will apply the style to your chart.

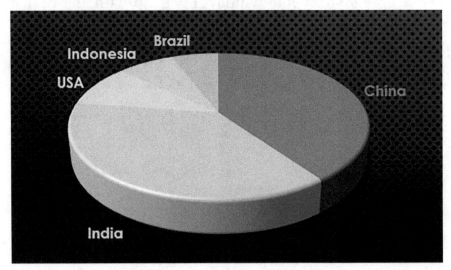

Chart Colour Schemes

You can also change the colour schemes (the colours used to represent the different data in your chart).

Sometimes the colours aren't as clear, so having the ability to choose different colour schemes helps with clarity and makes your chart stand out a bit more on your slide.

To do this, click on your chart to select it.

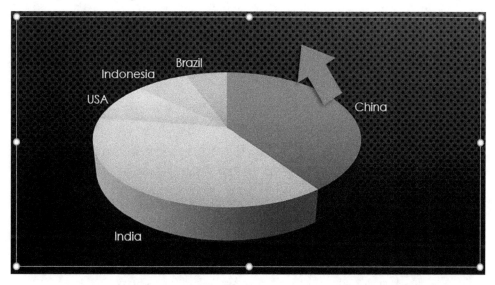

From the design ribbon under 'chart tools', click 'change colors'.

From the drop down menu, select a colour scheme that shows up your chart clearly and matches the colours of your slide.

Transitions and Animations

In this section, we'll take a look at adding transitions and effects to spice up your presentations.

Before we begin, throughout this section, we will be using the resource files.

You can download these files from

www.elluminetpress.com/ms-ppt

Go down to the files section and click the icons to download the documents to the documents folder on your PC.

Slide Transitions

A slide transition is an animation or effect that is displayed when you move from one slide to the next.

To add transitions to PowerPoint slides, click the slide you want to add the transition to, then go to the transitions ribbon.

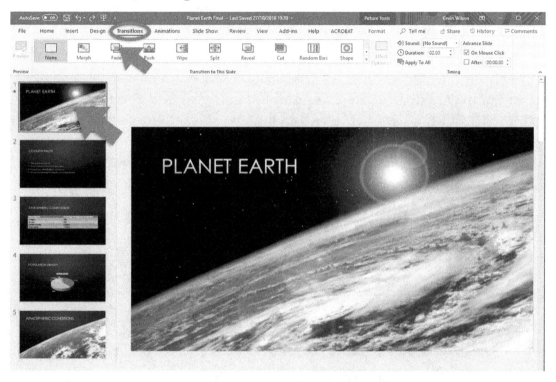

From the transitions ribbon, you can select from several pre set transitions. If you click on a transition, for example 'fade', this will apply the transition to the selected slide.

You can change the duration of the transition. The current duration is 0.7 seconds. If you want a slower transition, increase the duration. Try 1 or 2 seconds.

You can tell PowerPoint to wait for a mouse click to transition to the next slide, or you can make PowerPoint transition to the next slide after a set time. On the far right of your transitions ribbon, use 'on mouse click' to transition to next slide when you click the mouse, or un-check 'on mouse click' box and adjust the timer where it says 'after' with the length of time to display the slide.

To apply the transition to the whole presentation, click 'apply to all' on the right hand side of the ribbon.

Morph Transitions

The morph transition allows you to animate objects from one slide to the other. You can use text, shapes, pictures, charts, WordArt, and SmartArt.

To use the morph transition, you'll need two slides with at least one object appearing on both. The best way to achieve this is to create one slide with all the objects in the start position, then duplicate the slide and move the objects into the finish position. First slide morphs into second slide.

Create a new slide. In this example, I'm going to add the three planets, venus, earth and mars. This is the slide with all the objects in the start position of the morph animation.

Now, duplicate the slide. This slide has all the objects in the end position.

On the duplicate slide, move and resize the objects into the end position. You can also add more objects. I'm going to add a text box to show the stats for planet earth

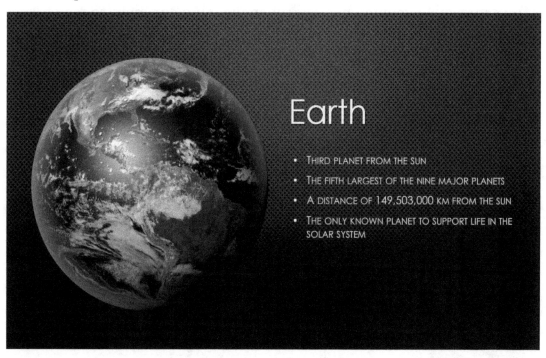

On the transitions ribbon, select morph.

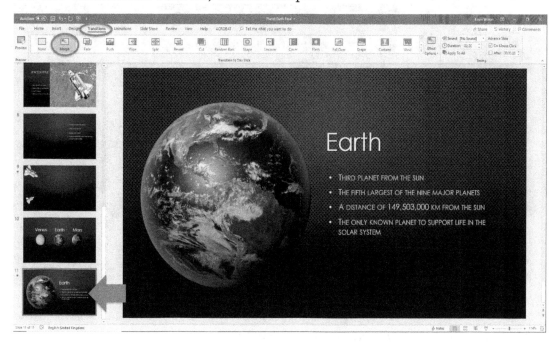

Watch the two slides transition into each other. Click 'preview' on the left hand side of the transition ribbon to see the morph.

Animations

You can add animations to slides to move text boxes, make bullet points appear, animate shapes and so on. This can help to make your presentation flow so objects and text appear at the right time while you're presenting. Animation effects can also help to emphasise certain points.

Effects

Looking at the slide below, say you wanted each bullet point to appear one at a time, instead of all at once.

You can do this by adding an animation to the text box. Click into the text box and select your animations ribbon.

For this example, I am going to add a fade effect. To do this, select 'fade' from the animation pre sets circled above.

Try one of the other effects and see what happens. You can apply an effect, in the same way, to any object, photo, textbox, heading or logo.

Motion Paths

A motion path is an animation effect that allows you to move an object such as a photo, shape or text box across the screen.

To create a motion path, first click on the object you want to animate. For simplicity's sake, I'm going to use a circle. Go to your animations ribbon, click 'add animation' and select 'lines' from the motion path section of the drop down menu.

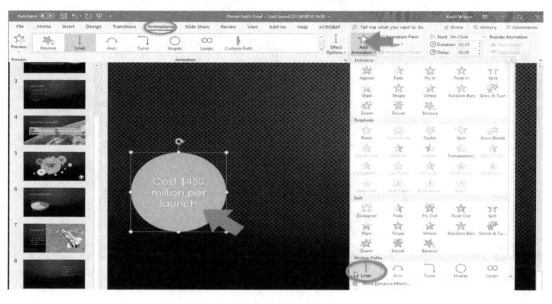

Now, if you look really closely, you'll see two very small dots on the light blue circles. One dot is green, this is the starting point. The other dot is red, this is the end point.

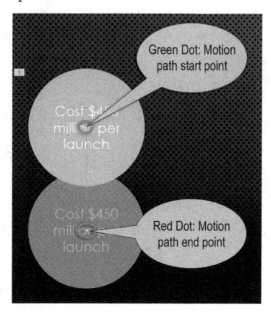

Chapter 6: Transitions and Animations

To create a motion path, you need to drag the green dot to the point you want the object to start at, then drag the red dot to the point you want the object to end up.

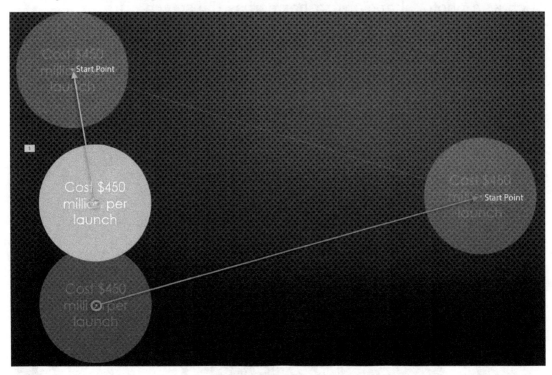

If you click 'preview' on the top left of your animations ribbon, you'll see the circle move left to right across the screen.

You can apply this effect to any object, textbox, photo or heading. You can also use different paths: arcs, turns or loops, and manipulate them in the same way, by moving the start and end points. Try an arc, to move the path, drag the resize handles on the box around the arc path.

So you end up with something like this... you can see the motion path arc down then back up in a 'U' shape.

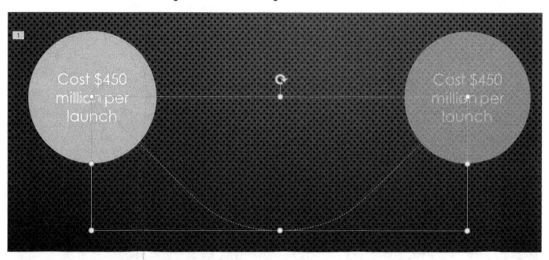

If the resize box disappears, click back on the motion path.

Custom Motion Paths

You can also draw your own paths if you prefer. Click on the object you want to animate. Go to your animations ribbon, click 'add animation'. From the drop down menu, go right down to the bottom and click 'custom path'.

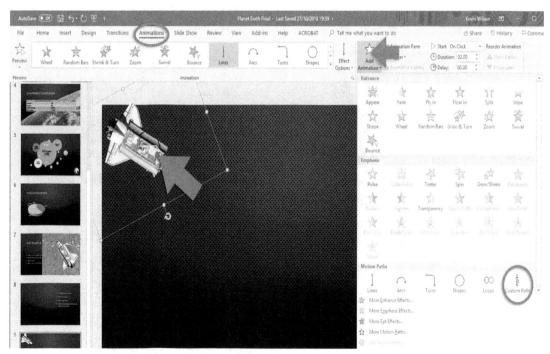

Now draw the path on the slide with your mouse. Highlighted below in red.

Double click on the position on the slide you want the object to end on.

Now, when you preview your slide, you'll see the ship fly to the bottom right corner.

If you double click on the path you have just drawn, you can make some adjustments to the speed and the timing.

Effects & Timings

You can adjust the timings. Set a 'smooth start' means the shape will start to move slowly then accelerate to full speed as it moves across the screen. Similarly 'smooth end' means the shape will gradually slow down as it nears the end of the motion path, rather than stopping suddenly.

'Bounce end' allows you to add a bounce effect to the shape when it gets to the end of the motion path - you can get the shape to bounce in a similar way to a ball bouncing on a hard surface.

Change these by entering the number of seconds into the boxes in the effect tab.

On the timing tab, you can set the trigger that starts the shape moving. Change this in the 'start' field. On mouse click is usually best to start your animation if you are presenting to an audience.

You can also set a delay before the animation begins with the 'delay' field, enter the number of seconds.

You can change the duration of the animation using the 'duration' field. This slows down or speeds up the animation on your shape.

You can set the animation to repeat a set number of times or until you click the mouse again, using the 'repeat' field.

Animation Pane

With the animation pane you can view and manage all of the animations that are on the current slide. From here you can adjust timings and the order of your animations.

In this slide, we have two images, note their names: 'Picture 8' and 'Picture 2' as listed in the animation pane. Next to the object names in the animation pane, you'll see a blue bar. This is a timing bar and indicates how long the animation on that particular object is. The left hand side of the bar indicates the start while the right hand side of the bar indicates the end of the animation. You'll see a meter right at the bottom of the animation pane showing the number of seconds.

By default, PowerPoint will play the animations one at a time as listed in the animation pane. So for example, in the slide above, the animation on 'picture 8' will play, then when that animation is finished, the animation on 'picture 2' will start.

You can change the length of the animation by dragging the right hand edge line of the blue bar to the right, in the animation pane. You'll see the number of seconds on the end increase.

You can get the animations on the objects to start at the same time. On the animations pane, the first object in the list has a small mouse icon next to it, this means that the animation on that object will start when the user clicks the mouse.

Right click on the second object in the list and from the drop down menu, click 'start with previous'.

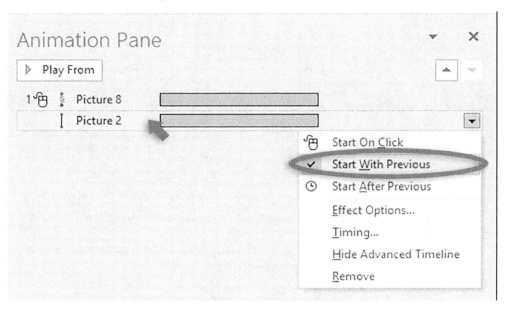

Now both animations will start at the same time. If you wanted 'picture 2' to start a bit after 'picture 8', drag the left hand edge of the blue bar next to 'picture 2', to the right. You'll see some seconds. This is the amount of time before the animation on this object starts. In this example, 'picture 2' will start 1.6 seconds after the user clicks the mouse.

Picture 8 will start as soon as the user clicks the mouse.

This is useful if you have a sequence of objects that need to appear at different times during the slide animation.

Adding Multimedia

In this section, we'll take a look at recording and adding audio, narrations, and video clips.

Before we begin, throughout this section, we will be using the resource files.

You can download these files from

www.elluminetpress.com/ms-ppt

Go down to the files section and click the icons to download the documents to the documents folder on your PC.

Adding Video

You can add videos from your computer and videos from an online video sharing source such as YouTube.

Add Video on your PC to a New Slide

To add a video to a new slide, click 'new slide' from your home ribbon. From the drop down menu, click 'content with caption.

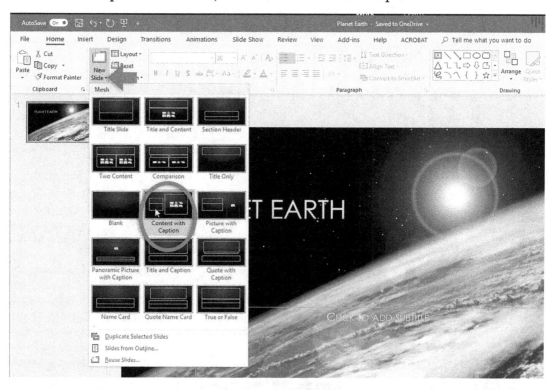

On the new slide, click the 'insert video' icon

Select 'from a file', then from the popup dialog box, navigate to the folder on your computer where your video is saved. In this example, the video is in the 'videos' folder.

Double click on the video you want to add.

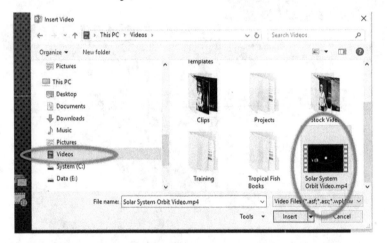

Add a title and some bullet points to your slide and here we go.

Add video from your PC to an Existing slide

If you already have a slide that you would like to add video to, go to your insert ribbon and click 'video'.

From the drop down click 'video from my pc'. Select 'online video' if you are linking to a YouTube video.

From the dialog box, double click the video you want to insert.

You may need to resize your video, if you don't want it to fill the screen. You can do this by clicking and dragging the resize handles on the edges of the video.

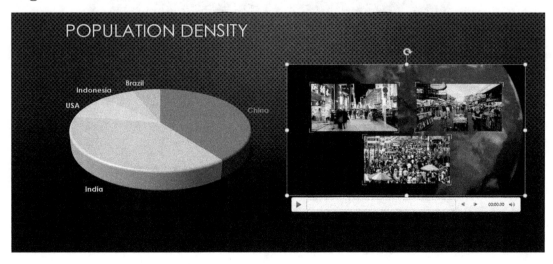

Trimming Videos

You can trim videos to start in exactly the right place. You can't do this with online videos yet, but you can trim any that have been downloaded to your computer.

Click on your video and from the playback ribbon, click 'trim video'.

From the popup dialog box, drag the start point towards the right (indicated in red, above), to the point where you want the video to start. You'll see a preview of the video at the top of the dialog box.

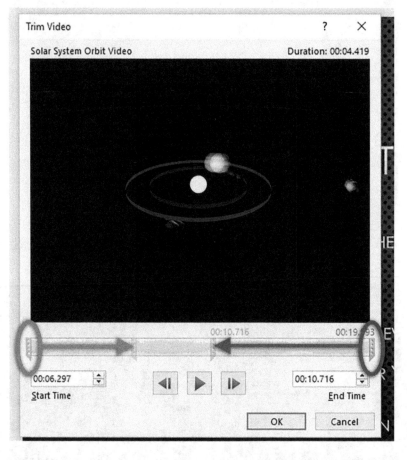

Do the same with the end point. Drag the end point to the left (indicated in blue, above), to the point you want the video to stop.

Click OK when you're done.

Online

You can link to YouTube videos from your slide. Insert a blank slide, then from your insert ribbon click 'video'. From the drop down menu select 'online video'.

From the popup dialog box, go down to YouTube, and in the search field type in what you're looking for. In this example, I'm looking for a video to go on my space shuttle page, so I typed 'space shuttle launch'.

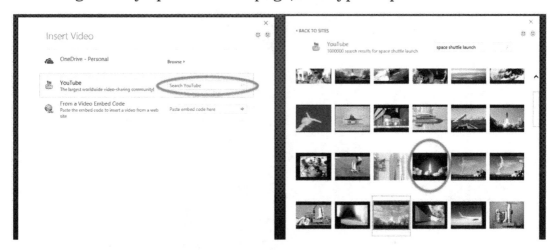

Double click on the video thumbnail in the search results to add the video to your PowerPoint slide. You might need to resize your video and move it into position on your slide. Add some information about it too.

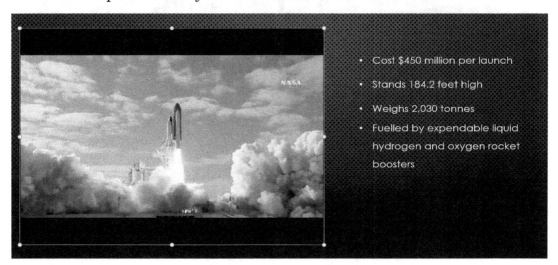

Adding Sound

You can add audio files that contain music or voice as well as record your own audio.

Recording Audio

To record audio, the first thing you should do is invest in a good microphone, especially if you intend to use your recordings as voice overs or links in a recorded presentation. This will vastly improve the quality.

The mic pictured below is a fairly inexpensive option.

This type of microphone will plug directly into a USB port on your computer or laptop with little or no configuration, which makes it ideal for PowerPoint presentations.

This comes in handy for recording narrations and presentations. We'll cover this a bit later.

Audio from your PC

If you already have a slide that you would like to add audio to, go to your insert ribbon and click 'audio'. From the drop down click 'audio on my pc'.

From the dialog box that appears, browse to the audio file you want to insert. In this example, my audio is stored in my music folder.

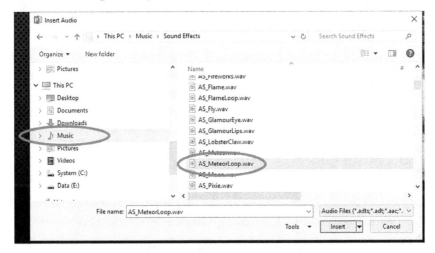

Your audio will show up as an icon on your slide.

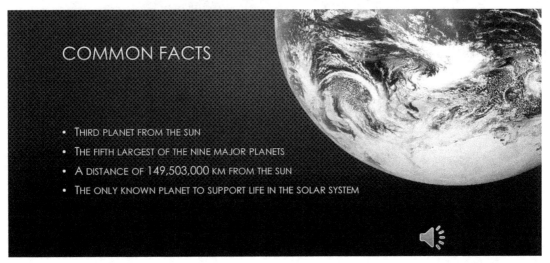

By default, you'll need to click the icon when showing your presentation to start the audio.

To change the audio settings, click on the audio icon on the slide

Select the 'playback' ribbon under 'audio tools'.

From here you can listen to a preview, trim the audio clip so it starts and ends in specific parts of the track.

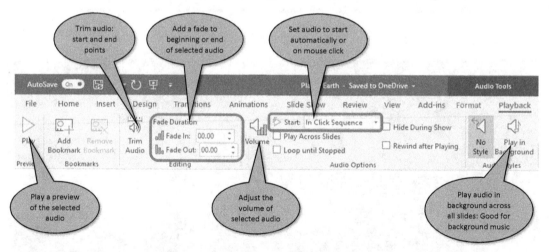

You can add a fade in effect, so the audio fades in at the beginning and fades out to silent at the end, using the 'fade duration' options.

You can change whether you want the audio to play in one slide or across all your slides using 'play in background' option.

You can choose whether your audio plays automatically or if it starts when you click your mouse. You can adjust this using the 'start' setting on the audio options.

Screen Recording

Screen recording is useful if you are demonstrating something on your computer, or training someone to use a piece of software.

First, select a slide or insert a new one, then select your insert ribbon. From the insert ribbon click 'screen recording'.

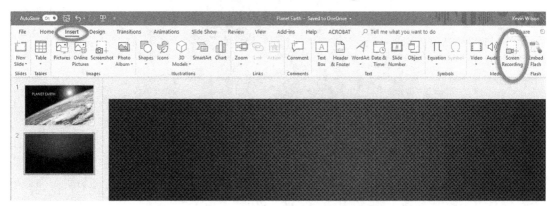

You will need to select the area of your screen you want to record. To do this, click and drag the selection box across the part of your screen to record, eg, click the top corner and drag your mouse across the screen, as shown below.

If you want the whole screen, click the top left corner and drag your mouse all the way to the bottom right corner.

When you have done that, click 'record' to start recording.

You'll get a 3 second countdown before you begin...

When the countdown hits zero, start the demonstration of what you're recording. PowerPoint will record your mouse clicks, applications opened and so on, within the area you selected in the previous step.

To stop recording, hold down Windows & Shift Key, then tap 'Q' - don't hold 'Q' down.

Your recorded screen video will appear in the selected slide. You may need to trim the screen recording because it's useful to remove the bits at the beginning where the control box is showing and at the end, so the screen recording just shows what you intended.

To do this, click on the screen recording video and from the playback ribbon click 'trim video'.

Now click and drag the beginning and end markers on the timeline to the points where you want the recording to start and where you want it to end.

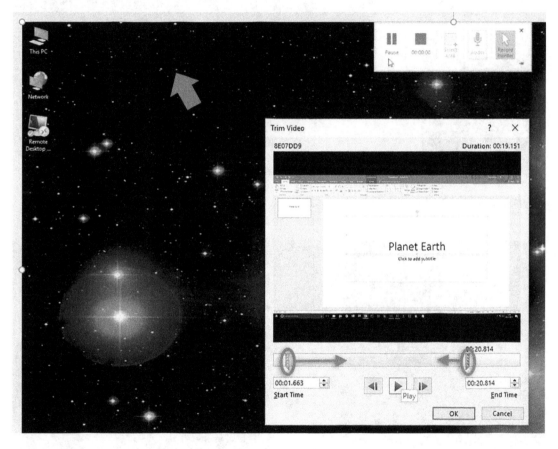

Click OK when you're done.

Recording Presentations

Record slide and animation timings, along with narrations, so the presentation will run through automatically.

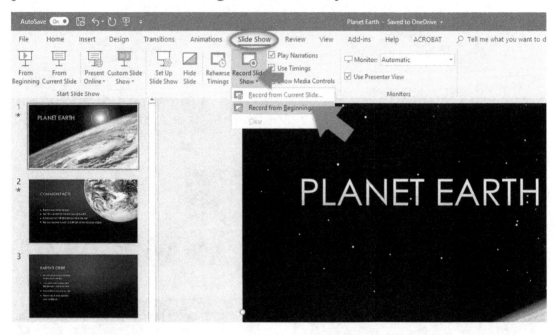

If you want to record narrations, click settings and make sure 'record audio' is checked and PowerPoint has found your microphone.

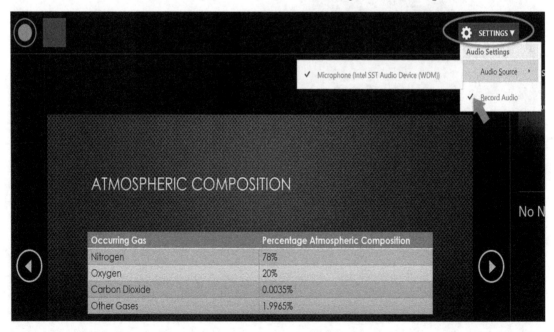

When you're ready, click the red button on the top left of the screen to start the recording.

Now give your presentation as if you were presenting to an audience, speaking into your microphone. It's best to be in a room where it is fairly quiet and with no echoes.

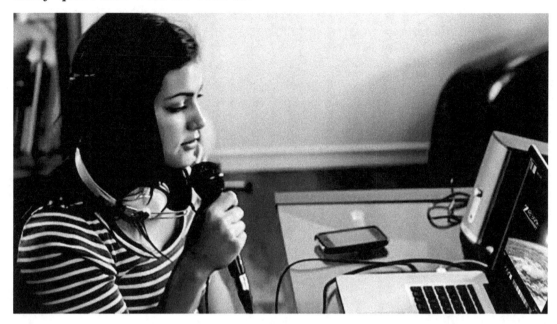

You can also use the screen annotation tools to draw on the slides, highlight points etc. PowerPoint will record your screen annotations, animations, bullets and transitions as you go through your presentation.

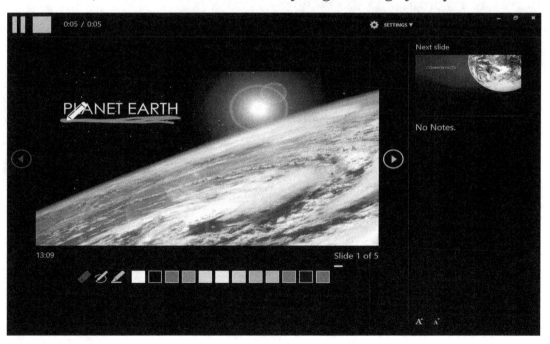

Once you are finished, click the stop button (large grey square on the top left).

Export your Presentation

You can export your presentation as a video file and upload it to YouTube or social media. This will include all your slide timings, transitions, animations, as well as your narrations.

Click File, then select export.

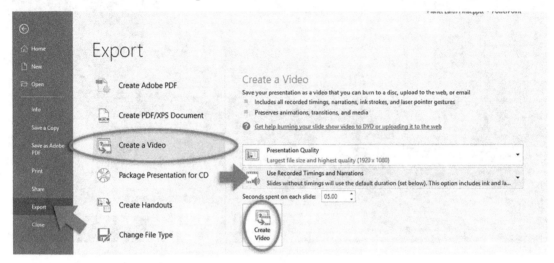

Set the presentation quality to the highest setting and select 'use recorded timings and narrations' to include your slide timings, annotations and narration recordings in the video.

Click 'create video', then select the folder you want to save it in. I'm saving my video in the 'videos' folder. Click 'save'.

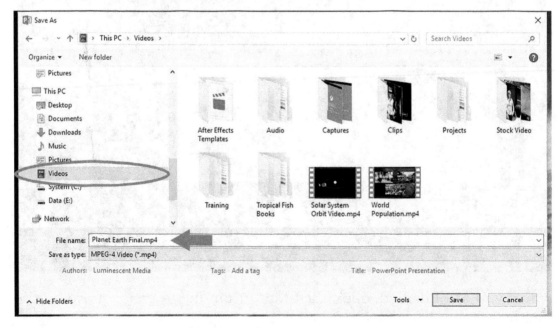

Photo Albums

There are two ways you can create photo albums. You can use the album generator on the insert ribbon, or you can use a photo album template from office.com.

First, lets have a look at some of the templates available on office.com. Go to FILE and click NEW.

Type 'Photo Album' into the search field. You'll see a list of templates appear in the search results.

Double click on one of the template thumbnails to open a new presentation with that template.

Now you can start adding your images to the photo place holders in the presentation.

If there is a sample image already on the slide, to change it, right click and from the popup menu select 'change image'. From the slide out, select 'from file'. This is for photos stored on your computer.

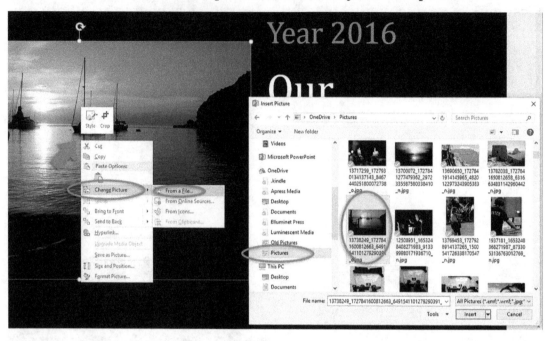

On the slides, you'll see image place holders already laid out on the slides. To add an image, click the image icon in the middle.

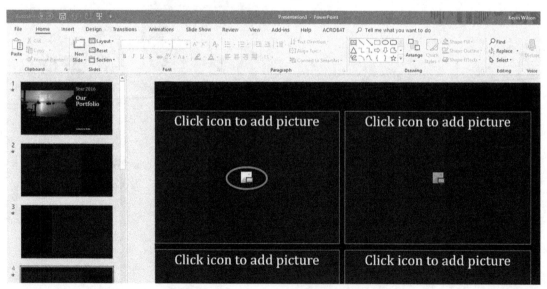

From the popup dialog box, select the image you want to insert. Do this with all the image place holders on all the slides.

You can also change the layouts of the photos. For example, on the second slide, say you wanted six small photos instead of one large photo.

To change the layout, click 'layout' from your home ribbon and select the layout from the drop down menu.

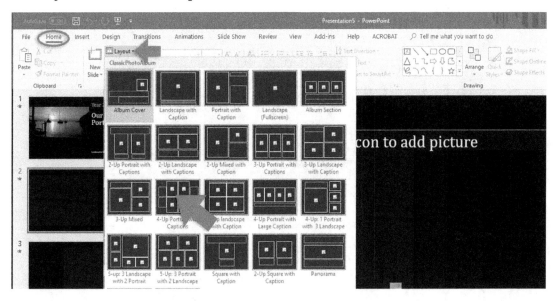

You can also add slide transitions as with ordinary slides, as well as animations for your photographs. To add animations, click your photo.

If you want to select more than one photo, hold down your control key while you select your photos.

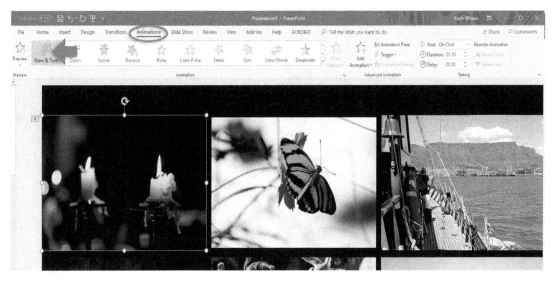

From the animations ribbon, select an animation pre set. Do this with all the images you want effects on.

You can also create a photo album using the album generator on the insert ribbon.

Go to your insert ribbon, and select 'photo album'.

From the 'photo album' dialog box, click 'file/disk'.

Then from the 'insert new pictures' dialog box, navigate to your pictures folder, or where your photos are stored, and click to select the ones you want. If you are selecting more than one photo, hold down the control key while you select your photos.

Click 'insert' when you're done.

You can also select a pre designed theme. To do this, click 'browse',

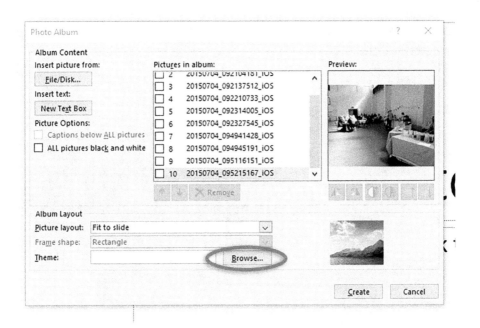

From the 'choose theme' dialog box, choose a theme from the list.

Click 'select' when you're done.

You can arrange the photos, one to a slide, more than one to a slide, or you can arrange to a slide with a title or caption.

To do this, click 'picture layout' and select an option. I'm going to select '1 picture with title'.

When you're done, click 'create'.

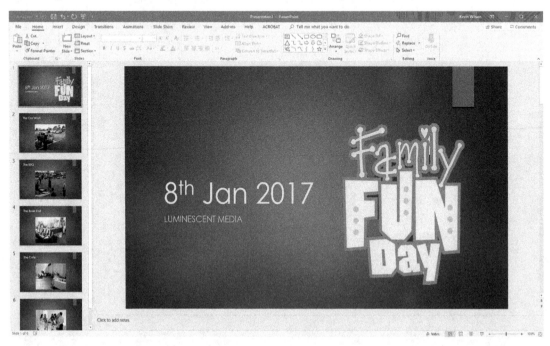

Now you can change the titles, add clipart and arrange the photos on your slides just like in any other PowerPoint presentation.

Edit your slides, add captions, headings and animations to your slides to make your album more exciting and interesting to watch.

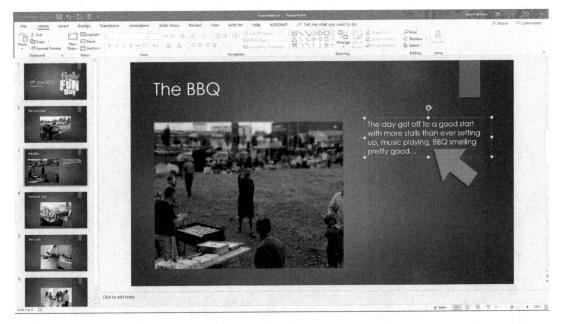

Run your photo album in the normal way. Press F5 on your keyboard.

Microsoft PowerPoint Pen Support

In Microsoft PowerPoint, you'll see an additional ribbon menu called 'draw'. This has all your drawing tools such as pens, highlighters and an eraser for you to annotate your presentations.

Select the 'draw' ribbon and select a pen colour from the selections in the centre of the ribbon. From here you can select the colour and thickness of your pen.

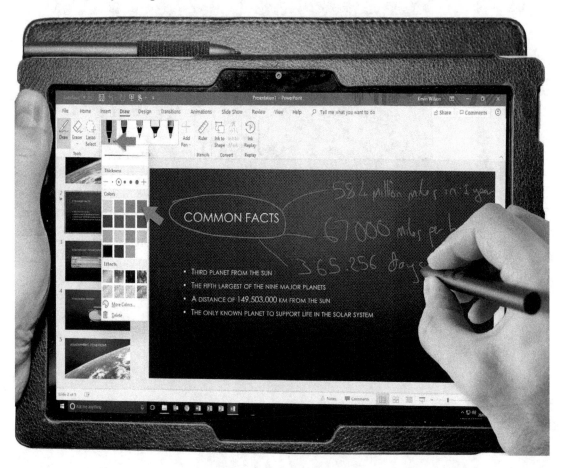

You can annotate and draw on your slides in preparation for your presentation and when you save your presentation, PowerPoint will save your drawings and annotations as well.

You can also use your pen tools while you are presenting.

All your annotations and illustrations will appear on your presentation for your audience to see.

PowerPoint will also give you an option to save your annotations added during your presentation.

You can then save the presentation with all the annotations and highlights as well as share these with colleagues or friends.

To share, click the share icon on the top right of your screen.

Enter the email address of the person to share the presentation with, then click 'share'.

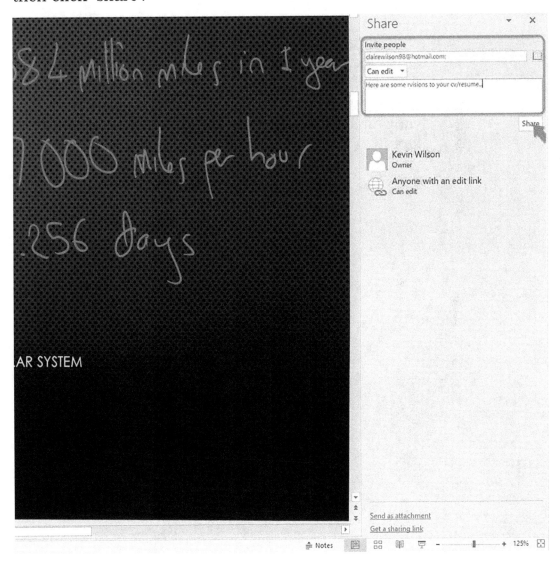

The other person will get a link in an email they can click on to view or edit the presentation.

Giving Presentations

In this section, we'll take a look at setting up to give your presentation using projectors, tablets or your laptop.

Setting Up Projectors

Connect your laptop to your projector. Modern projectors either use a VGA or an HDMI cable to connect. The projector in the example uses a VGA, but the principle is the same regardless of what cable you're using.

Connect the other end to your laptop

DVI

Digital Video Interface is a video display interface used to connect a video source (eg your computer) to a display device, such as an HD ready TV, computer monitor or projector.

HDMI

High Definition Media Interface, is a combined audio/video interface for carrying video and audio data from a High Definition device such as a games console or computer to a high end computer monitor, video projector, or High Definition digital television.

Pictured below is Standard HDMI & Micro HDMI.

VGA

Video Graphics Array is a 15-pin connector found on many computers and laptops and is used to connect to projectors, computer monitors and LCD television sets.

Plug the power lead into the projector.

Now fire up the projector. Once the projector is running, start up your laptop.

On your laptop, the best way to use PowerPoint is to use an extended screen display. This means that the projector screen is an extension of your laptop screen, rather than a duplicate. This will allow you to have notes and to see the next slides coming up in your presentation - the presenter display.

In Windows 10, to do this, hold down the windows key then tap 'P'. From the side panel that opens up, click 'extend'.

Running your Presentation

The controls for running your presentation can be found on the slide show ribbon.

On the right hand side of the ribbon, click the drop down box next to 'monitor' and select the name of your second screen or projector.

This tells PowerPoint, which screen to display your presentation on for your audience to see. Your laptop or tablet screen is your presenter view. This will show you any notes you have written as well as the next slide. If you want this feature, tick 'use presenter view'.

To run your presentation, click 'from beginning' icon on the left hand side (or press F5). This will run your presentation from the first slide.

You have a few useful tools available while you present (circled in the image above).

You can zoom into a specific part of the slide to highlight it, by clicking the magnifying glass icon and positioning the rectangle over the part of the slide you want to show.

You can annotate your slides with notes to help your audience understand your point. Click the pen tool, select the pen and draw on the slide with your finger, a stylus or a mouse.

You can also present with a Windows 10 tablet running PowerPoint connected to a projector.

You may need a mini display port to VGA adapter, or a USB3 to VGA adapter to connect directly to the projector.

Wireless Presenting

If you're using Windows 10, there is a feature that allows you to project to another Windows 10 device. So you could have your Windows 10 laptop hooked up to the projector and use your Windows 10 tablet to wirelessly project to your laptop.

Both your laptop and tablet will need to be on the same wireless network for this to work. Some laptops wont support this, but most modern ones do. To connect, on your tablet open your action centre and tap 'connect'.

Your Windows 10 tablet will scan the network for your laptop... In this demo, the laptop's network name is 'Asus-Laptop' and the tablet's name is 'surfaceone'.

Once found, you'll see your laptop appear in the search results. Double tap on the name to connect.

On your laptop click 'yes' on the connection prompt that will appear on the bottom right of your screen.

Once you click 'yes', you'll see a blue screen on your laptop while your devices connect.

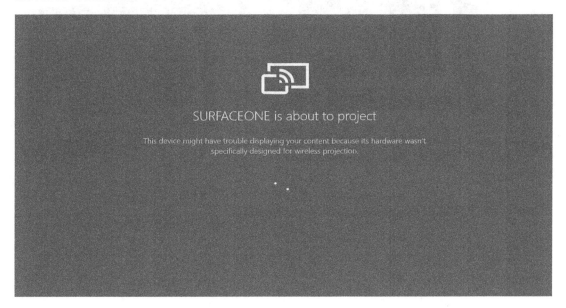

If you're having trouble, make sure your laptop is set up to receive. Go to your settings icon on the start menu, click system, then click 'projecting to this PC'.

Projecting to this PC

Projecting to this PC

Project your Windows phone or PC to this screen, and use its keyboard, mouse and other devices, too.

Windows PCs and phones can project to this PC when you say it's OK

Available everywhere ⌄

Ask to project to this PC

Every time a connection is requested ⌄

Require PIN for pairing
◯ Off

This PC can only be discovered for projection when it is plugged in
◯ On

PC name   Asus-Laptop
Rename your PC

Make sure your laptop supports wireless projection, and that the settings are set up as shown in the screen above. Also check your wifi settings on your laptop and tablet.

Now you can start PowerPoint on your tablet and you'll see the screen project to the laptop.

With the laptop connected to your projector, you're all set to present with a wireless tablet.

You can remote control the laptop from your surface tablet and present wirelessly, using the ink features of PowerPoint to highlight important points and concepts you want your audience to take note of.

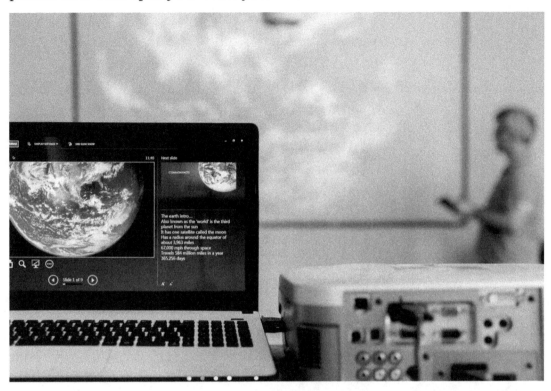

You can now use PowerPoint on your tablet and run your presentation.

You can use the touch features on your tablet, such as a stylus and annotate your slides as you present.

Present Online

You can set up a presentation and present it online, so anyone with a link to your presentation can 'tune in' and watch.

To do this, open your presentation and from the slideshow ribbon, click 'present online'.

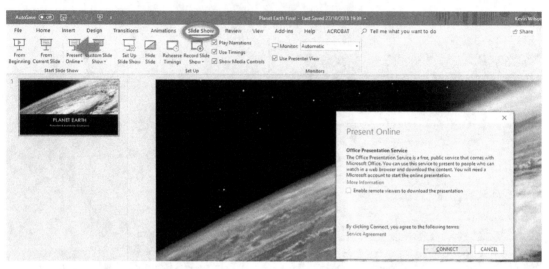

From the dialog box that appears, click 'connect'. *If you want your audience to be able to download a copy of your PowerPoint presentation, click the 'enable remove viewers to download the presentation'.*

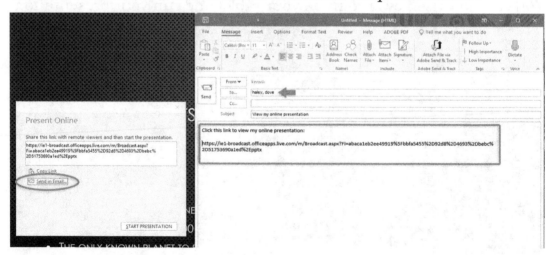

Next, invite the people you want to see your presentation. If you have Outlook installed on your machine, click 'send an email'. Add the email addresses to the email message that pops up. You can also click 'copy link' to copy to your clipboard and paste into sms/text message, imessage or skype.

When you are ready to begin, click 'start presentation' to begin your broadcast.

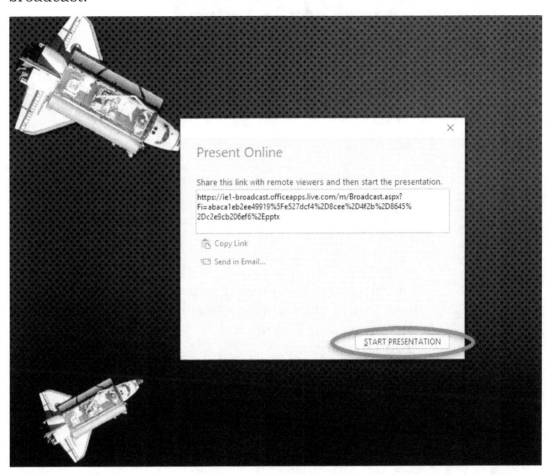

In the demonstration below, the laptop on the left is hosting the presentation.

The iPad and the Surface Tab are viewing the presentation in a web browser. These could be anywhere with an internet connection.

Resources

To help you understand the procedures and concepts explored in this book, we have developed some video resources and app demos for you to use, as you work through the book.

To find the resources, open your web browser and navigate to the following website

www.elluminetpress.com/ms-ppt

At the beginning of each chapter, you'll find a website that contains the resources for that chapter.

File Resources

To save the files into your OneDrive documents folder, right click on the icons above and select 'save target as' (or 'save link as', on some browsers). In the dialog box that appears, select 'OneDrive', click the 'Documents' folder, then click 'save'.

The sample images are stored in a compressed zip file. To download the zip file, right click on the zip icon on the page above, 'Sample Images. zip. Select 'save target as' (or 'save link as', on some browsers) and save it into 'pictures' on your OneDrive folder.

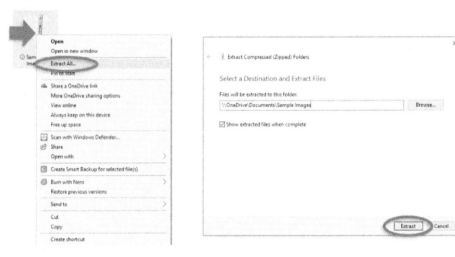

Once you have downloaded the zip file, go to your 'pictures' folder in your OneDrive, right click on the zip file, and select 'extract all' from the menu. From the dialog box that appears click 'extract'. This will create a new folder in your pictures called 'sample images'. You'll find the images used in the examples in the books.

Video Resources

The video resources are grouped into sections for each chapter in the book. Click the thumbnail link to open the section.

Getting Started

Building Documents

Managing Documents

Images, Tables & Charts

Document Templates

When you open the link to the video resources, you'll see a thumbnail list at the bottom.

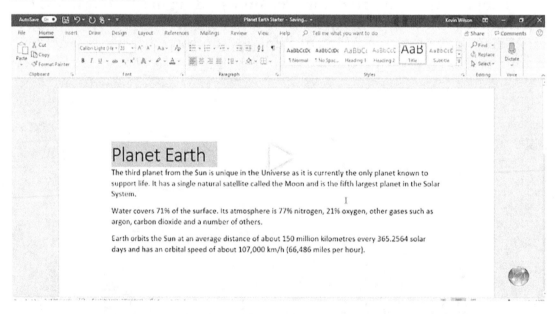

Click on the thumbnail for the particular video you want to watch. Most videos are between 30 and 60 seconds outlining the procedure, others are a bit longer.

When the video is playing, hover your mouse over the video and you'll see some controls...

Index

Index

V

W

DISCARD

9 781913 151058